Things I Wish I'd Known

Before We Became Parents

Things I Wish I'd Known
Before We Became Parents

GARY CHAPMAN

with SHANNON WARDEN

NORTHFIELD PUBLISHING
CHICAGO

All Scripture quotations, unless otherwise indicated, are taken from the Holy Bible, New International Version®, NIV®. Copyright © 1973, 1978, 1984, 2011 by Biblica, Inc.™ Used by permission of Zondervan. All rights reserved worldwide. www. zondervan.com. The "NIV" and "New International Version" are trademarks registered in the United States Patent and Trademark Office by Biblica, Inc.™

Edited by Elizabeth Cody Newenhuyse
Gary Chapman photo: P.S. Photography
Shannon Warden photo: Picture This Photography
Interior design: Smartt Guys design
Cover design: Faceout Studio and Erik M. Peterson
Cover image of mobile copyright © 2015 by IconicBestiary / iStock (77362511). All rights reserved.

Library of Congress Cataloging-in-Publication Data

Names: Chapman, Gary D., 1938- author.
Title: Things I wish I'd known before we became parents / Gary Chapman with Shannon Warden.
Description: Chicago : Moody Publishers, 2016. | Includes bibliographical references.
Identifiers: LCCN 2016023890 (print) | LCCN 2016027118 (ebook) | ISBN 9780802414748 | ISBN 9780802494764 ()
Subjects: LCSH: Parenting--Religious aspects--Christianity. | Child rearing--Religious aspects--Christianity.
Classification: LCC BV4529 .C434 2016 (print) | LCC BV4529 (ebook) | DDC 248.8/45--dc23
LC record available at https://lccn.loc.gov/2016023890

We hope you enjoy this book from Northfield Publishing. Our goal is to provide high-quality, thought-provoking books and products that connect truth to your real needs and challenges. For more information on other books and products that will help you with all your important relationships, go to 5lovelanguages.com or write to:

Northfield Publishing
820 N. LaSalle Boulevard
Chicago, IL 60610

1 3 5 7 9 10 8 6 4 2

Printed in the United States of America

To our spouses,

Karolyn Chapman and Stephen Warden,

with whom we have shared the joys

and challenges of parenting.

CONTENTS

Preface

A few years ago I wrote *Things I Wish I'd Known Before We Got Married.* I have been so encouraged by the response to that book. Many counselors and pastors have made it a part of their premarriage counseling for young couples. Many parents and grandparents have given it as a gift. I continue to believe that if we did a better job of preparing for marriage, we would be more successful in creating a healthy marriage.

I believe the same is true in rearing children. The better prepared we are, the more likely we are to be good parents. From the day that book was written, I knew that someday I wanted to write a sequel: *Things I Wish I'd Known Before We Became Parents.* As Karolyn and I struggled in our marriage in those early years, we also struggled in rearing our two children. No one told us what to expect, and no one told us what to do. Fortunately, we did our best, and both of our children made it to adulthood and have established healthy marriages, and we now have two grandchildren.

When the time came to write the book you hold in your hand, I knew that I wanted to coauthor with someone who still had young children and could speak out of recent experience. When Dr. Shannon Warden expressed interest, I was thrilled. A number of years ago Shannon was on staff in our counseling office. She returned to graduate school, earned her PhD, and for several years has taught counseling on the college campus, currently at Wake Forest University.

Shannon is married to Stephen and has three children: Avery, Carson, and Presley, whom you will meet in the following pages. She has learned how to balance marriage, children, work, and church responsibilities. She speaks not from the academic tower but from the trenches of real life. In the introduction you will get to know Shannon's journey to motherhood. She has experienced the trials and joys of pregnancy and rearing children.

I am grateful to have Dr. Warden join me in writing what I believe to be a much-needed book. Our desire is to share our own experiences, as well as what we have learned through the years, as we have counseled hundreds of parents. We encourage you to read this book before the baby comes, and then refer to its chapters again as you experience the joys and challenges of rearing children.

GARY CHAPMAN, PhD

Introduction

Preparing for parenthood takes a lot of time and energy and often begins well before pregnancy. Couples may discuss the best time to get pregnant. They sometimes think about changes they need to make in terms of their relationships, work schedules, incomes, houses, cars, etc. In this introduction I have asked Shannon to share her journey to parenthood. I think her story will reveal why I asked her to join me in writing this book.

S tephen and I chose Avery's name about three years before he was born. We were excited to think about and begin planning our family. We first conceived after nine months of trying, but I miscarried within a couple weeks of a positive pregnancy test. Stephen and I were already confused as to why it was taking so long to get pregnant, even though we had read that approximately 10 percent of women have trouble getting or staying pregnant.[1] Although the miscarriage was an emotional setback, we did not give up on our dream of having a child.

When finally pregnant with Avery, we were hopeful and anxious. Hope grew as I did, and our attention turned from the anxiety of whether I would miscarry again to other attention-getters that many moms-to-be experience—nausea, fatigue, swelling, difficulty sleeping, indigestion, hemorrhoids, moodiness, depression, anxiety. Information and support from medical professionals, family members, and friends were extremely valuable in dealing with these and other physical and emotional stressors. Soon the excitement of ultrasound pictures, baby showers, and fun activities such as decorating the nursery helped make pregnancy more bearable. Eventually Avery arrived, and we were overjoyed.

About three years after Avery was born, Stephen and I began trying to get pregnant with a second child. We did not know what to expect, but, based on our first pregnancies, we knew it might take some time. After a few months of trying, I got pregnant, only to learn at the ten-week ultrasound that I had miscarried, likely in the sixth or seventh week. Disappointed but hopeful, we then waited the recommended few months and began again working diligently to get pregnant—with no results for more than a year. We finally consulted a fertility specialist with whom I did some months of unsuccessful fertility treatments.

As time wore on, Stephen and I grew more discouraged and confused. The fertility specialist recommended in vitro fertilization, something I knew had benefited so many couples. But I did not want to go that route. I told Stephen, "I think God is saying, 'I will give you a baby in My timing.'"

What I did not know, of course, was that He already had. I was pregnant with our son Carson at that very moment, as I would discover a couple weeks later when my pregnancy test read positive.

By the time Carson turned a year old, Stephen and I were feeling fairly successful in terms of maintaining work/life balance.

We felt successful enough that we decided to have a third child. Before making that decision, we consulted with friends and family who have three or more children. All said it was hard; all said it was worthwhile; and all said they would not have done a thing differently. Interestingly, this time around, Stephen and I got pregnant almost immediately with no fertility issues, and nine months later Presley arrived. We still marvel at how easy it was to get pregnant with Presley as opposed to getting pregnant with Avery and Carson. We count this as a reminder about life and parenting—that you can't always predict what will happen, but you can always find hope in your circumstances.

Shannon and Stephen's parenting journey is not atypical. However, every couple is unique, but always there will be joys and challenges. The same is true for couples who cannot or choose not to get pregnant but choose adoption instead. There certainly exists much need in the world for loving adoptive parents. Similar to birthing biological children, adoptive parents experience their share of uncertainty, stress, and joy through the adoption process. Here again, great intentionality, planning, and flexibility are required to be as prepared as possible to parent children, whether they are biological or adopted.

Although pregnancy can seem to last forever, the months steadily pass by, and it is time for your baby's debut in the world. Of the various birthing options (e.g., vaginal delivery, delivery by Caesarean section, delivery in a hospital birthing center, home birth), all naturally seem at least somewhat complex and messy. Similar to pregnancy, women are wise to be both flexible and as informed as possible about the choices and challenges involved with childbirth. Even after being as prepared as possible, you, like many parents, will discover that television deliveries and friends' stories will not fully prepare you for the birth of your own baby. Your story will, in fact, be uniquely yours—uniquely challenging and uniquely wonderful. The good news here is that, no matter the complexity, mess, and pain of birth, great joy awaits you just seconds after your baby's birth—the joy of holding and kissing your precious bundle of joy for the first time.

Perhaps the joys and challenges of awaiting the arrival of your new addition will help prepare you for the joys and challenges that lie ahead. Wherever you may be on the continuum—contemplating parenting, trying to get pregnant, expecting your first child, exploring adoption options—it is our hope that the following chapters will remind you of the many pleasures and benefits of parenting and encourage you to remain hopeful and positive even in hard parenting moments and seasons.

You will quickly identify a central theme throughout the book—that parenting is worth it! It is worth the uncertainty and stress of getting pregnant, the discomfort and pain of pregnancy and childbirth, and all of the other stresses thereafter that parents face. We believe parents know this instinctively, yet we believe that encouragement and information can be a helpful resource to parents. So read for hope, for laughter, for reassurance, and for reminders of the little and big things that make parenting worth your time and energy.

1

I Wish I'd Known . . .

That Having Children RADICALLY CHANGES *Your* SCHEDULE

I remember the Sunday morning our daughter was born. I woke up to hear Karolyn saying, "I'm having contractions." "What does that mean?" I asked. "I think the baby is coming."

"Really?"

"Yes, I think we need to go to the hospital."

So I quickly dressed and we were off to the hospital. I had never experienced having a baby, nor had she. We were both excited, but more than a little naive.

We had been married three years and we were ready to have a child, or so we thought. We had always planned to have children. When we were dating, Karolyn said that she wanted to have five boys. (She was from a large family.) I was "in love" so I said,

"Whatever you want is fine with me."

I had no idea what I was saying.

However, on that morning I was ready for our first one. We did not know whether it would be a girl or a boy. I know this is hard to believe, but this was before ultrasound machines. Until the baby came out of the birth canal, one never knew. I must confess this added to the excitement.

Another thing you will find hard to believe is that in those ancient days, husbands were not allowed to be in the delivery room. I think the nurses got tired of catching fainting husbands. So, it was deemed best if they stayed in the waiting room. In fact, the doctor said to me, "It is going to be several hours, so I think if you would like, you can go back to the church and preach your sermon and then come back; you will have plenty of time." (He knew that I was pastor at a small church in town.) I was shocked at this suggestion, but thought, "Why not? I can tell the congregation about the good news."

> We discovered that having a baby and caring for a baby are two different things.

So I did. At the end of the sermon, I said, "I will not be at the door to greet you this morning because earlier this morning I took Karolyn to the hospital. The baby should be coming soon, and I am going back to the hospital." I sensed that the ladies were upset that I had not stayed at the hospital, but after all, I was simply following the doctor's suggestion.

At any rate, when I got back to the hospital, all was calm in the waiting room. Ten minutes later, the nurse burst into the room and said: "Congratulations, you are the father of a baby girl." I followed her into the delivery room where I saw our baby lying on Karolyn's stomach. She said, "It's a girl, but I couldn't help it."

It is amazing what people say in moments like that. I said, "That's fine, you're the one who wanted boys, I'm happy with a girl." The doctor said, "She will have him wrapped around her little finger in no time." He was right about that!

Two days later we went home with our baby. That is when we discovered that having a baby and caring for a baby are two different things. All those late-night trips to the Dairy Bar to meet Karolyn's craving for a banana split were much easier when the baby was in her womb. In fact, everything was easier when the baby was in her womb. Now, the baby had to be fed far more often than I had imagined. Karolyn chose to breastfeed for the first several months. I suggest you talk with your doctor, mother, and friends who have walked this road as you make this decision. Breastfeeding does seem to be nature's way, but there are often issues involved. What you want is what works best for you and your baby.

Then, there is all that mess that happens at the other end of the baby's body. That too happened far more often than I had imagined. In those "good ole days" we used cloth diapers that had to be washed. Not a pleasant task. We opted for a diaper service. They took the dirty diapers and brought them back clean. Of course, now most couples use disposable diapers—much easier. However, it still takes time, and the smell is not pleasant.

These are the basics: put the food in, take the food out. If you don't do this, the baby will not live. While these two are necessary, there are all those other hours that must be devoted to the rearing of a child. We hope that as an infant, they will sleep several hours of the day and night. If this happens, you are fortunate parents. This will give you time to cook meals, wash laundry, mow grass, and all those other necessities for adult life together.

Our daughter slept much more than we had anticipated. Even so, we felt compelled to look at her while she was asleep to make sure she was still breathing. We did not know how good we had it until we had our second child, a son, who did not want to waste time sleeping. So he took much more of our time.

We knew the value of tenderly holding our baby. I had read all the research about babies who go hours without tender touch and how their emotional development is hampered. We wanted our baby to feel loved, so we held her often and talked and laughed with her. As she got older we read stories to her long before she understood our words, because we wanted to stimulate her brain with pictures and sound. We wanted to be good parents.

However, all of this took time—much time. In theory, we knew that a child would demand much of our attention, but theory and reality are very different. I wish someone had told us that we would have to change our schedules after the baby arrived.

We had already made one major decision before the baby arrived. Karolyn decided that she would like to be a stay-at-home mom. So we agreed that she would quit her job before the baby was born. With that decision made, I assumed that I would not need to make many changes in my schedule. After all, a "full-time mom" should be able to handle the baby, right?

> A willingness to admit your limitations and adjust your schedule will keep you from feeling defeated or disappointed with yourself.

I was in for a rude awakening. There is a reason why it takes a mom and a dad to create a baby. There is a reason why in marriage we commit ourselves "to love and to cherish" each other. Never will love be more needed than when you have a child. All research indicates that the healthiest setting in which to raise a child is that created by a mother and father who have a loving, supportive attitude toward each other. My earlier book *The 5 Love Languages*[1] has helped millions of couples create such a loving, caring, supportive relationship. With this kind of relationship, both are willing to adjust schedules to meet the other's needs and the needs of their children.

Another important factor is recognizing our limitations. We cannot do everything. All of us have limitations. A father cannot work out in the gym two hours each day, hold down a full-time job, spend three hours at night on the computer, attend a sports event, or play golf every Saturday and be a loving husband and father. A willingness to admit your limitations and adjust your schedule to include those things that are most important will keep you from feeling defeated or disappointed with yourself. Time, money, energy, and abilities are all limited. Achievable goals lead to celebration when accomplished. Unrealistic goals may lead to depression when we fail to reach such goals.

Important also is developing or maintaining a "we" mentality. Hopefully, even before the baby comes you have shifted from the "I" mentality, which most of us have before marriage. This shift much be made permanent. Parents can no longer think in terms of what "I" am going to do but rather what "we" are going to do. Parenting is a team sport.

Self-sacrifice is another required attitude in making scheduling changes. My coauthor, Shannon, was doing a counseling internship as part of her doctoral training. She met a hospital chaplain who had a PhD degree and had taught at a local university for several years. She explained that she had loved being a mother and intentionally slowed down her career during her children's childhood so that she could be with them as much as possible and still work. In higher education, this meant that she didn't climb up the tenure ladder as quickly as she might have. For her, parenting was more important than the professional ladder.

Whether it is at work or in other areas of life, parents often experience personal or professional sacrifice to some degree for the sake of their children. Sometimes this sacrifice feels more pronounced; other times parents would not even call it sacrifice.

Adjusting our attitudes and choosing how we will approach parenting is a worthwhile but challenging task. However, living with unrealistic, unachievable expectations and resulting disappointment is undesirable and unproductive.

Making it work

In addition to attitude changes, we also need to take practical steps if we are going to cope with the time demands of being a spouse and parent. Shannon and I have put together the following suggestions, which we feel will help you make needed schedule changes.

1. *Get organized.*

We know this is problematic for two reasons. First, not everyone is gifted with the ability to organize. This is one of the realities I discovered after I got married. I am extremely organized and my wife is the opposite. Second, it takes time to get organized, and time is one of the limitations we are dealing with in the first place.

However, there are small changes you can make that will pay great dividends. Take a look at your present schedule and ask: What do I anticipate that I might need to change after the baby arrives? Or, if the baby is already in your home, identify the pressure points, and ask: How could I lower the pressure by organizing my time differently?

Maybe you could wake up thirty minutes earlier. Maybe you can work in a half-hour walk during your lunchtime. Maybe you can give your spouse a break by washing the dishes.

2. *Get creative.*

Your baby will not always be a baby. Sooner than you can imagine you will be doing creative things with them, such as playing pirates or having tea parties. Coloring books will again return to your life. These are just a few examples of the creativity that naturally happens in parenthood. Parents also have to call upon their creative thinking when faced with managing busy family schedules.

Multitasking can be creative, but it may not always be the best for your child. When you are able to take your child with you as you do a routine task such as grocery shopping, you are both accomplishing a necessary task and also exposing your child to a stimulating environment. However, when you are talking with your child while you are sending a text or doing some media-driven activity, you are cheating your child of quality time.

3. *Involve others.*

Parents often cannot be with their children 24-7 and need the help of trusted others to care for their children. Some parents are fortunate to have family or friends nearby who can help with childcare. Quality nurseries, preschools, and grade schools also play important roles in the lives of some families. Parents may be reluctant to seek help with childcare, especially first-time parents who are anxious about leaving their child for the first time. All parents are wise to explore childcare options and thoroughly evaluate the safety and trustworthiness of those options. With such effort, and as parents build trust in those caregivers, they gain not only a sense of relief but also a sense of freedom. As one friend said, "I love taking my kids to daycare!" She meant that both as a compliment to the daycare facility and as a personal expression of freedom to accomplish her other responsibilities. She, like many parents, knew firsthand that it truly is a blessing to have help in raising your child.

Shannon and Stephen were fortunate enough to have family nearby. Grandparents are happy to have time with grandchildren (as long as it does not get too long or too often). Karolyn and I did not have parents nearby. However, we had some wonderful friends who were willing to babysit for an hour or so while we did a task. Other wonderful single adult friends stayed with the children as they got older and allowed Karolyn and me to attend conferences and take short trips.

4. *Simplify.*

Any way you slice it, life with children gets hectic. And it gets more hectic as they get older. Once the ball games and piano and dance recitals start, life can become a marathon. At some juncture you will need to simplify. What activities can be eliminated? Life should not be constantly pressured. The human mind and body need rest and time to be free to think, and enjoy the simple things like a sunset, a rainbow, or a bird. One parent said, "This is the first Saturday in a long time that we have nothing to do." Strive for more Saturdays like that!

When our baby was little, Karolyn found that Sunday evening was a wonderful time to relax with the baby. As a pastor, I had Sunday evening responsibilities, but I encouraged her to stay at home. Did all of the congregation understand? No! But most of them did because they stayed at home also. Culture, even Christian culture, should not control our lives. We are responsible to God and not to culture.

5. *Celebrate what's working.*

Look for opportunities to affirm each other. By focusing our attention and energy on what is going right, we not only encourage and connect with our spouses and children in more positive ways, we also have an improved perspective on what's not working. We feel like our wins overshadow our losses, and we believe we can work through other challenges that we face.

This list of ideas is certainly not exhaustive. However, these ideas may serve as a useful starting point as you begin actively identifying your family's schedule strengths and limitations. I wish someone had shared these ideas with me before we became parents.

Talking It Over

1. Have a conversation with a couple who gave birth to a child in the past six months and ask how the baby changed their schedule.

2. If both of you are currently working full-time, have you discussed whether or not you will make vocational changes after the baby is born? Have you made any decisions yet?

3. If each of you decides to continue your full-time vocation, what childcare options do you anticipate?

4. Make a list of the major activities each of you does with your "free time"—such things as golf, gym routine, video games, hobbies, Facebook, etc. Do you anticipate cutting back on any of these after the baby arrives?

5. Make a list of the normal household chores that are done on a regular basis and who presently does each of them. List such things as purchasing groceries, cooking, washing dishes, sweeping or vacuuming the floor, cleaning the toilet and shower, etc. Do you anticipate changing roles on any of these?

6. How willing are you to make personal sacrifices for the benefit of your child?

2

I Wish I'd Known . . .

That Children Are **EXPENSIVE**

A few days after our daughter was born, I received the invoice from the hospital. The total cost for her delivery was nine dollars. (Remember, these were "the good old days," and we had good insurance.) A baby for nine dollars, you can't beat that deal! I must confess I was elated. I really don't think that it ever crossed my mind to contemplate what it would cost over the next twenty-six years as we watched her progress through elementary school, middle school, high school, college, and medical school. Frankly, I'm glad, for it may have overwhelmed me.

However, if you are the planning type, and you really want to know, you may want to look at the annual report of the United States Department of Agriculture's Center for Nutrition Policy and Promotion (CNPP) report entitled: "Expenditures on Children by Families."[1] I'll give you the bottom line. The estimated cost to raise a child from birth through age seventeen is around $250,000. This figure is based on a middle-income, two-child, husband-wife family. This does not include costs related to college, or other expenses after the child turns eighteen years old. (I know, some of you have already turned to your calculator and figured out that is $14,705 per year.) Of course, costs can greatly vary depending on housing, food, transportation, clothing, health care, childcare, education, and many other factors.

I hope that doesn't discourage you, but if it does, then take a black magic marker and black out the above paragraph. In fact, few couples sit around contemplating the long journey. I know that we did not. Life is to be lived one day at a time. We give birth to our babies and then fall madly in love with them so much so that we instinctively commit ourselves to figuring out how to afford the costs they create. Hopefully, common sense will kick in and tell us when we are spending more than we are making. This reality calls for a course correction.

One of the decisions Karolyn and I made early on was to "live within our means." Neither of us likes debt. So we did not even own a credit card until our baby was born. We moved to Texas for graduate school a few months later and needed a crib. We applied for a credit card and were turned down because we had no credit record. In retrospect, failing to establish a credit record was not a good idea. Again, one of those things I wish I'd known. Of course, getting a credit card today is much easier. In fact, you can't walk through an

> I have come to view children not as an expense but as an investment.

airport without voices calling out who want to give you a card.

The wise use of credit cards (paying the balance each month when due) can make life much easier. However, building up debt on a credit card has led many families into serious financial problems. Hopefully the ideas we share in this chapter will help you live within your means as you rear your child.

As we go along we discover that children not only cost us financially, but as we began discussing in chapter 1, children also cost us time and energy. Money, time, and energy! All that cost may sound pretty discouraging, but I have come to view children not as an expense but as an investment. In fact, I believe children are our best "investment." They bring us great joy in those early years. We love them, and they learn to love us and love others. We help them discover and develop their unique interests and abilities. Then they grow up to bless the world and enrich the lives of those they encounter. If we maintain a loving relationship, then in our old age, they care for us as we become more childlike and they, more adult. What could be a better investment?

Certainly the value that children add to our lives and to the world far outweighs any financial cost. However, it is helpful and practical to anticipate the costs they create and decide how wisely to budget finances, time, and energy so that you are best able to care for your child.

Neither Shannon nor I are financial experts. We often encourage our clients to seek consultation with financial advisors when in need of more thorough financial strategies. However, we have found a few common principles to be helpful to parents who share with us their financial struggles. These principles are: 1) commitment to self-discipline is essential; 2) organization is helpful; and 3) creativity stretches dollars. I wish I had known these before Karolyn and I became parents.

Commitment to self-discipline

One definition of self-discipline is governing oneself for the sake of improvement. The first step in self-discipline is to become aware of what changes need to be made. When applied to finances, it means we keep records of how we use our money so we can discover if we are living within our means. If we are not able to pay our regular living expenses without going in debt, then it is time for a course correction. This calls for a discussion of: how can we cut our expenses, or how can we make more money? Once we make these decisions, self-discipline calls us to strictly abide by our decisions.

Shannon shared that when she and Stephen realized they needed a course correction they committed themselves to things like: "eating out less and cooking healthier but simpler meals at home; taking our lunch to work; buying less on impulse and more for need rather than desire; and spending less on credit." She continued, "Like so many couples, we previously tended to focus more on our day-to-day desires and use convenience and perceived need as an excuse to spend somewhat frivolously at times. By renewing our commitment to financial self-discipline, we found new and rewarding ways to save money for the more important things. These improved strategies not only freed up more money to pay for our children's short and long-term needs but also strengthened our relationship with each other. This was an unexpected bonus."

Karolyn and I really had to learn self-discipline when I returned to graduate school. We had one child, and we agreed that Karolyn would not work outside the home. I had a part-time job at a local bank where I made enough to pay our rent, utilities, and basic food needs. There was nothing left over. I remember the day that Karolyn said to me, "Honey, would you mind paying the bills and balancing the checkbook each month?" This was a task she had agreed to do. I asked, "Sure, but why?" "Because it hurts my stomach," she said. That shows you how tight the money was.

There was literally nothing left over for clothes, fancy meals, or recreational activities. I look back with deep appreciation for Karolyn's self-discipline. Three years later, we left graduate school with my PhD degree and no debt. She did not buy a pair of shoes for three years. Now that our children are grown, you know why I never complain when she comes home with six pairs of shoes.

Each couple will need to decide what they can do to "make it" financially. Once they agree on the decision, then self-discipline is required to reach their objectives.

Organization is helpful

By nature, I am an organized person. You can look at our dishwasher after I have loaded it and know that I am an organized person. Karolyn, on the other hand, loads a dishwasher like she was playing Frisbee. However, when it came to our finances, I was not nearly as organized. Yes, I paid the bills each month (after I was conscripted), and I balanced the checkbook, but I had never written out a budget. As noted above, a budget is a very helpful tool in organizing your financial assets. Another of those things I wish I'd known before we became parents.

I must confess that the budget idea did not kick in until after the graduate school days. But once I had a real job, and we had a little more money, putting everything on paper in categories became an eye-opener to me. Karolyn and I became aware that we needed to think ahead a few years when our daughter would likely go to college. This forced us to think more clearly and specifically about what we were doing with our money.

Shannon and Stephen had a similar experience. "When Stephen and I got more serious about money management, we realized that his strategy of 'spend less, save more' was no longer good enough. My optimistic outlook of 'we'll make it work' was no longer good enough. We had to get more organized in our bookkeeping so that we knew our exact expenses and could anticipate budgetary needs. Stephen worked up a much more thorough budget with my input, and then we discussed how we might best manage our discretionary income each month. This was a giant step forward for us."

She continues, "For many years we lived as if finances would just handle themselves. We now are much more organized in our handling of finances so that we are more unified in our efforts to operate within our budget."

Other organizational skills include such things as making a shopping list before you go to the grocery store. This may keep you from impulse buying and save you many dollars. Or having clearly in mind how much money you have to spend for clothes before you go to the store. With this amount in mind, you are more likely to buy out of need rather than fleeting desire.

There are only three things that one can do with money: spend it, save it, or give it away. Before we got married, Karolyn and I both agreed that we would invest 10 percent in Christian endeavors. We both took our faith seriously and believed that this was a way of honoring God. However, we were not as specific about what we would save. It was after we had a child, and I finished grad school, that we agreed to save 10 percent of our income. This was one of the wisest decisions we ever made. Thus, in order to live on the remaining 80 percent, we had to be creative, which brings us to our third suggestion.

Creativity stretches dollars

Some women are masters when it comes to creative cost saving. They make their own baby food, soap, and clothes. They shop with coupons and sell at consignment stores. They recycle common household objects to make useful gadgets and toys. These are all wonderfully creative cost-saving strategies. Shannon admits that she does none of these, but still considers herself to be creative.

"Stephen and I have saved many of Avery's clothes so that Carson has a ready supply of clothes, thus preventing us from having to fully reoutfit Carson each year. We watch the DVDs we already own and do not feel compelled to always buy new ones. We play in our neighborhood and go to public parks. We fly kites and ride bikes and tricycles. We buy clothes for ourselves that we can mix and match rather than overstocking our wardrobes with clothes we will rarely use. These are a few of the things we do to creatively stretch our dollars. Again, I am not the most creative or the thriftiest, but small savings are still savings. We are simply trying to be more practical and creative in our spending and saving."

When you have a girl and then a boy, you cannot pass clothes along. However, Karolyn found a friend who had a boy a few years older than our son who loved the opportunity to pass along his clothes to our son. Don't worry about your son getting a complex from wearing hand-me-downs. It is an excellent way of teaching him that we always want to make the most of whatever we have. Service to others is a high virtue. We also accepted toys from others and then passed them along when our children outgrew them.

We spent hours with our children doing things that cost nothing, such as playing active games outside and board games inside. When they were smaller we colored many books with crayons. We read books to them from the time they were able to sit in our laps. Consequently, both of our children grew up with a love for reading. While riding in the car, we "counted cows" as we drove through the country. (For you city dwellers, you can count cars or buildings.) We often told them stories from our childhood, about the games we played and the things we did. Karolyn would take them to the library each week when they were old enough. They learned how to check out books and pieces of art, which we would hang on their bedroom walls. There is no limit to the creative things you can do with your children that cost little or nothing.

Karolyn never buys clothes for herself unless they have been marked down at least three times. She has high-end tastes, but gets them at low-end prices. I never ask her how much she spent, but rather, "How much did you save us today?" Creativity is your friend when it comes to cost saving.

You can also be creative in "making money." We never did this, but I have heard many parents share their experience of teaching young children how to make cookies or cupcakes and selling them at a craft fair. This is both teaching them a skill and the principle of working in order to make money.

Other stay-at-home moms make real money sewing or selling online. Again, creativity is a friend to one who wants to bring more money into the family.

Managing time and energy

Self-discipline, organization, and creativity are not only helpful in terms of financial strategies, but they are also helpful with managing time and energy. Many new parents have little understanding of how little time they will have for themselves once their sweet newborn makes his or her debut. Then, fast-forward a bit, and that sweet baby becomes a toddler who naps less, and then a school-aged child who not only has school but also extracurricular activities. Parents' days suddenly are filled not only with their typical work schedules and personal agendas but also with cleaning up after their children, grocery and clothes shopping, and transporting their children from one place to another.

The busyness of parenting is not bad. In fact, we have never once heard a parent say, "I wish I had spent less time with my children." Instead, parents tend to cherish time spent singing, reading books, acting out stories, building and knocking down castles, racing Matchbox cars, painting pictures, playing outside, or whatever other fun activities children enjoy. This is time well spent, and time that so many parents miss when their children are older. With that perspective in mind, it may be easier for parents to appreciate the privilege of rearing children rather than begrudge the time children demand. At the same time, parents need time to keep their own relationship alive.

One of the decisions Karolyn and I made was to have a specific bedtime for our children. When they were little, bedtime was seven o'clock. When they turned six, and started school, we gave them five extra minutes. Each year we moved bedtime back five minutes so at twelve years of age it was seven thirty. When they became teenagers, we jumped it to nine o'clock. Of course when they got in high school things changed. With basketball, piano recitals, and extracurricular activities, our goal became ten o'clock. When it became bedtime, they did not have to go to sleep, but they had to go to their room. They could read a book until they were sleepy. (No television was allowed in the bedrooms.) Our children got plenty of sleep and thrived in school. It also gave us some "couple time" each evening.

I know that contemporary parents are saying, "How do we get them off the screens of modern technology?" The answer is simple. You control the technology, and don't let it dominate the life of your children. Have screen-free zones in the house; for example, no screens in the bedroom. Have time limits on the screens. Control what is watched. (For more help in how to do this, see my book *Growing Up Social: Raising Relational Kids in a Screen-Driven World.*[2]) Children adapt easily to structured living, but parents must set the boundaries.

Closely related to the amount of time parenting requires is the energy that is required of parents. Both Karolyn and I have a rather high level of energy. Energy is renewed by sleep, exercise, and relaxation. We did not feel a severe drain of energy with the birth of our daughter. As I mentioned earlier, she slept much of the day and night. So, we were able to sleep. It was after the birth of our son, who thought sleep was a waste of time, when we began to find our energy running low.

Again, self-discipline, organization, and creativity helped us find ways to maintain energy levels so that we could play with the children, manage their schedules along with our own, plus respond to their ever-expanding and ever-changing emotional needs.

The first step in self-discipline was to evaluate what was needed so that we could maintain energy to do all of this. Karolyn's desire to be a stay-at-home mom made this much easier for us. She could take the night shift so I could get sleep, and she would get her naps during the day when the children took their naps. As the children got older, I would take them to the nearby park in the afternoon so she could have some time alone. I found that if I was stressed at work, a ten-minute stop on the way home just to sit in the car and relax, or take a short walk, prepared me to let the stress go and get ready for the adventure at home.

Once parents decide their priorities, it takes self-discipline to order our lives in keeping with these priorities. We must consciously decide to budget time in order to maintain energy to accomplish our objectives. Spending quality time with our children was one of our priorities. This meant that we had to say no to various professional or personal opportunities or per-ceived obligations to free up time to do this. Most parents want to spend more time with their children, and have time for each other. However, without self-discipline they may continue to overextend themselves in ways that sabotage their goals.

Organization and creativity can be your friend as you seek to balance the challenges of having children. Multitasking—interact-ing with the children while at the same time accomplishing other responsibilities—can sometimes be helpful. Shannon shares her own experience: "The floors in our house seem to stay dirty and require daily sweeping and vacuuming. Presley usually will not let me sweep unless she gets to hold the dustpan. I also have seldom vacuumed the house in the past ten years when not also carrying a child on one hip. Sweeping and vacuuming the house are work to me, but to the children, these tasks are fun. So, a creative solution to cleaning the floors while also spending time with the children is let them help me clean the floors. Does it take longer? Yes! But that does not matter. What matters is that I am accomplishing both my goals by involving the children in household chores."

She admits that sometimes multitasking is not always successful. "Sometimes I will look at my email while sitting in the play area or while holding Carson or Presley on my lap. Presley will push my phone away and pull my arms around her waist. Or Carson will start playing with my open laptop until I give up, close it, and return my focus to him. In these ways, they are communicating clearly that they want my undivided attention."

I am not suggesting that there is one right way to manage your time and maintain your energy. I am suggesting that without self-discipline, organization, and creativity you may find your life out of balance. One of the most common complaints Shannon and I hear in our counseling offices is, "I lost my spouse to the baby. We used to enjoy doing things together, but now it's like 'we' are no longer important. All our energy is given to the baby." This need not happen, but now is the time to make plans so that this does not happen. As the saying goes, "a failure to plan is a plan to fail." More about keeping your marriage alive in chapter 11.

So the question is, how will you organize your lives so that you have time, energy, and money to maintain a growing marriage, meet your own personal needs, and be good parents? Let me remind you that parents have been rearing children for thousands of years. With all of the technological changes we have seen in our lifetime, one would think that life would be easier. In reality, technology may well make your life more stressful. I believe that with self-discipline, organization, and creativity you can make technology your servant, not your master.

Time, energy, and money invested in your marriage, with your children, and maintaining your own physical, emotional, and spiritual health is time well invested.

Talking It Over

1. Were you shocked, discouraged, overwhelmed, or positive about the cost of rearing a child from birth through high school?

2. Are you presently committed to "living within your means"? If your answer is yes, how successful have you been to this point?

3. If you have debt, what is the total amount of debt and what are your plans for getting out of debt? This may include re-paying college loans. Be sure to include this in your budget.

4. Are you saving 10 percent of your take-home income? If not, what steps can you take to make that a reality?

5. Do you have a written plan (budget) that shows the monthly essentials, and how much is allotted for food, clothes, recreation, savings, giving, etc.? If not, why not begin the process by keeping records this month on where all your money went.

6. How disciplined are each of you in following a plan for handling your money once you have agreed on it? Does the thought of having a child motivate you to be more disciplined?

7. What creative ideas are you presently using to stretch your dollars?

8. As you anticipate becoming parents, are you open to exploring other creative ideas for getting more for your dollars? If so, you might consider the ideas in this chapter, or go online, or talk with other couples about what they have found helpful.

3

I Wish I'd Known . . .

That **NO TWO** Children Are **ALIKE**

We knew that all children are unique, but the tendency to compare our child with others was still very real. Of course, we knew that our daughter was more beautiful than others. We assumed that she was smarter than others. And we were committed to being model parents. The problem was that we had read no books on parenting, attended no parenting conferences, and had only vague ideas of what was involved in parenting. So, we naturally talked to other parents about their children, and got their ideas on how to be good parents. What we found was that the advice we received was conflicting. People had different ideas on how to rear children, and we discovered that not all children are alike.

Comparing our child to others, then, was not very helpful.

The comparison trap can cause a lot of unnecessary emotional struggle for couples. In addition to the conflicting advice of others, couples often discover that they have different ideas on how to parent their children. That is why empathetic communication is so important. We need to listen to each other as friends who are on the same team, not as competitors.

Not only do we compare our child to the children of other couples, we sometimes compare our own children with each other. This is unfair to the children and frustrating to the parents. The sooner we understand that no two children are alike, and that we must not try to force them to think and act alike, the sooner we are on the road to becoming good parents.

Too big? Too small?

Let's look at some of the areas in which children are unique. After the birth of the child, what is the first bit of information we share with family and friends? "It's a girl; 21 inches long and weighs 7.4 pounds." And what response do we get? "Oh, that is close to our baby. She was 20.5 inches and weighed 7.1 pounds." Of course, these are mothers who are having this conversation. Dads typically say, "It's a girl and she is healthy."

Size and weight are normally the first comparisons we make. The concerned mom and dad may ask themselves, "What is the normal weight for a baby?" Nothing wrong with that question, but the reality is that there is a wide range of "normal" weight. The normal range is from 5.5 pounds to 10 pounds. Ninety-five percent of all newborns fall within this range. If your child weighs less or more, it does not mean that they are in serious trouble, but it may mean that they will require special assistance. This is when pediatricians and neonatal nurses can be of great service.

It is common for an infant to experience a 5 to 10 percent loss of weight in the first few days after birth. Don't panic. This is normal. Karolyn and I did not know this and became somewhat concerned. Had we known this it would have saved calls to the pediatrician. Then, many children experience a growth spurt when they are seven to ten days old. Additional growth spurts may occur at three weeks and six weeks of age. The baby may demand extra feedings and may nurse longer. If mothers are not aware of this pattern, they may be asking, "What has happened to this baby?" Of course, these patterns may vary because children really are unique.

As the child gets older, size and weight may continue to be a concern for parents. For example, a mother may be concerned that her son is smaller than the other children in his preschool class. She may worry that he will be picked on, overlooked, or feel inferior because of his small size. Another mother may worry that her son's bigger-than-average size may cause others to stereotype him as having athletic talent that he may not possess.

Other parents may compare their child's body style and weight to other children's and worry that they are "too skinny" or "too fat," and that they may suffer with lower self-esteem because of their bodies. Concerns like these sometimes arise as early as infancy and can occur throughout childhood as children's bodies change. In dealing with size-related concerns, parents may want to consider consulting with medical and counseling experts as a way of gaining knowledge, perspective, and peace of mind. Such consulting may help to calm parents' unnecessary worries. In cases where concern is warranted, consulting may result in ideas for how you can help your child successfully navigate size-related challenges.

Modeling a positive attitude and positive handling of size-related issues cannot only help reduce parents' stress but also can greatly boost your child's self-esteem and positive problem-solving abilities.

The finicky eater

Another area in which children are unique is in eating habits. We noted above common patterns of weight loss and "growth spurts" in the early days. As the child gets older and is able to eat what we commonly call "baby food," the uniqueness of the child will become more apparent. Some children seem very interested early on in a broad variety of foods, whereas others are picky, or "finicky," about what they will eat. I still remember our son making a gruesome face and pushing away the spoon filled with green beans. On the other hand, he readily received the applesauce.

Shannon told me that her mother told her that her mother (Shannon's grandmother) took peanut butter and banana sandwiches to family reunions because she knew Shannon's mother would not eat otherwise. I must confess that as a child I loved peanut butter and jelly sandwiches. Bananas were fine too when they were available.

Regarding her own children, Shannon shares, "Avery was a finicky eater until about age eight, when he started being more open to trying new foods. Carson continues to be finicky, his favorite being peanut butter sandwiches with milk. We are excited that Carson is gradually expanding his interests to include new favorites: broccoli and corn. Presley so far seems to be naturally open to a broad range of foods, and so our food battles are far fewer with her than with our boys."

If we are honest, most of us as parents also have some foods that we are not fond of and seldom, if ever, eat. I won't name the foods I dislike, because they may be your favorite. We too are unique when it comes to food choices. Our grandson, who is in high school, still will not eat cheese unless it is on pizza.

So, what's a parent to do? My suggestion is expose your children to a variety of foods, but don't force them to eat what they dislike. A taste is fine, but don't force the whole jar of baby food on the child if they gag with each bite. Don't brag on one child because they eat their broccoli while the other does not. Hopefully you will discover enough healthy options to keep your child alive and thriving. Accept the reality that children are unique when it comes to food choices.

Is there a "right" amount of sleep?

A third area of uniqueness is sleep patterns. While all children need sleep, the amount of sleep and when they sleep may vary greatly from child to child. Our daughter slept eighteen hours a day. I was concerned that she was not getting enough physical and mental stimulation. I did not know that newborns typically sleep from eleven to eighteen hours a day. I wish someone had told me that before she was born. It would have allayed my fears.

Sleep is the primary activity of the brain during infancy. Sleep during the early months occurs around the clock and the sleep-wake cycle interfaces with the need to be fed and changed. Sleep rhythms begin to develop at around six weeks, and by three to six months most babies have a regular sleep-wake cycle. However, this cycle will differ with each child.

The key for parents is to learn the baby's sleep patterns and identify signs of sleepiness. Some babies will cry, while others rub their eyes. Most pediatricians recommend that you put the baby in the crib when you see signs of sleepiness, not after they have actually fallen asleep. This helps them learn how to get themselves to sleep, which often allows them to get back to sleep when they wake up during the night.

> "Most helpful to us was the reality that many of our friends' children didn't consistently sleep through the night."

At three to six months it is not too early to establish bedtime routines. Activities such as bathing, reading, singing, and praying done consistently and in the same order prepares your child for bed. Your baby will associate these with sleeping and they will help him or her wind down and fall asleep.

Often, by six months of age, babies will sleep through the night and no longer need nighttime feedings. Seventy to eighty percent will do so by nine months of age. Even when nighttime feeding is no longer needed, this does not mean that your children will sleep through the night. Don't be concerned if this is not your experience. Shannon notes, "None of our children slept through the night until they were about three years old. Maybe we should have known that this was a possibility beforehand, but we didn't. We consulted with various resources and tried with mixed success to change eating and napping habits. We occasionally made strides only to ultimately accept that restless nights are part of parenting. Possibly most helpful to us was the reality that many of our friends' children didn't consistently sleep through the night."

All of this affects the parents' ability to sleep. In fact, this is one of the earliest challenges parents face. They are already sleep-deprived from the first couple of days at home with their newborn and holding out hope that restful nights will soon return once their baby has adjusted to post-womb living. Then, parents realize that nightly feedings may cause a postponement to their hopes of restful sleeping.

If the mother is nursing, then the primary "night duty" falls upon her. The husband can help by trying to reduce her workload at other times so that she can get much-needed sleep. When nighttime feeding is no longer the issue, but the child is still waking up and needing attention, you can take turns being on duty to respond to the child during the night. If you have two small children, you may need to move to a "man-to-man" defense. If your child wakes up and continues to cry, you do need to respond. Your baby may be hungry, wet, cold, or even sick. Routine nighttime awakenings for changing and feeding should be as quick and quiet as possible. Don't turn on unnecessary lights or talk loudly or play with your child. Nighttime is for sleeping. Responding to your child's needs in this way models for them that parents love them and are invested in helping them no matter what. Such strong emotional bonds between parent and child outweigh the toll of a little lost sleep for the parents.

Yes, children have different sleep patterns—and so do the parents. Learning how to work together as a team so that everyone gets proper sleep can be a challenge, but it is necessary if we are all to remain healthy. No one can reach his/her potential without proper sleep.

Is my child sickly?

A fourth area in which children differ greatly is physical health. Some children are sickly and seem to often struggle with allergies, viruses, colds, earaches, etc. Other children seldom suffer from such symptoms. The reality is that some children have a stronger immune system than others, but all children get sick from time to time.

Shannon shares an experience not all that uncommon. "Stephen and I never knew prior to being parents just how much children vomit (gross subject, I know). We have cleaned up vomit from the bed, the car, the pool, and countless restaurants. And that's just 'normal' vomiting, not vomiting related to a disease." If you do not experience this with your child, count yourself fortunate. Children are unique.

It is never pleasant to watch your child suffer. Sickness also affects work and school schedules, which cause parents extra work and stress. When a child is sick, life cannot go on as normal. Parents are wise to plan ahead as to who will care for the child when sickness comes. The good news is that most childhood sicknesses are temporary and can be helped by medication and rest.

Unfortunately, medication and rest cannot always protect or cure children with severe allergies or chronic diseases. Parents whose children battle these types of problems must reach out for professional medical help. In these circumstances, parents may also experience guilt, shame, anger, depression, and other emotions, which can best be processed by sharing them with others. This may involve extended family, trusted friends, pastors, or counselors. Without the support and love of others, parents cannot be as effective in addressing the needs of their children. Wisdom always seeks help.

Strong-willed, easygoing, and more

One of the most observable differences between children is personality or temperament differences. Personality is our patterned way of responding to life. For example we hear people refer to children as "strong-willed" or "easygoing." These traits are observed early in the life of a child and are uniquely influenced by environment. And yes, each child is unique. However, there are categories that are commonly observed in children. We will look at just a few of these:

The first is *activity level.* Some babies and children are action oriented. In their waking hours they are constantly on the move. They are out to explore the world by crawling, then running and climbing. In their crib they are reaching for the mobile and continually moving their arms. On the other hand, there are those who are content to sit and play quietly. They explore the world through sight and sound. They are not constantly on the move. As they get older, they would rather read a book (if they have been exposed to books) than go play in the yard. If the parents are always on the go, they may be frustrated with their child who prefers reading over scaling the jungle gym.

A second category is *intensity of reaction.* Some children express their emotions loudly and clearly. They are highly intense about everything. If happy, they may laugh so hard and loud that you wonder if they are going to be an opera singer. If sad or angry, they may scream, throw things, or hit someone. To the parent they may seem to overreact to little things. Children on the low range of intensity tend to be quiet, rarely fuss, and sleep more than average. They have emotions, but do not express them nearly as strongly.

Third is *persistence*—attention span. Children who are persistent keep trying until they accomplish their goal. Those with a short attention span will give up and move on to something else.

Fourth is *reaction to new people.* You may want your infant to smile and coo when someone new enters their world. They may be more likely to stare stone-faced with a question mark in their eyes. Some toddlers will smile and even shake hands, but others may prefer hiding behind their parent rather than interacting with others.

The last category is *adaptability*—response to change. Some three-year-olds will race into their preschool class the first day and join in the play. Others will cry and hold on to their parent's hand. Some children will adapt quickly to the restaurant, while others will cry and refuse to eat. Some will have tantrums when you ask them to stop playing the game or turn off the TV. Others will adapt quickly and move on to the next event.

We could go on, but you get the idea. Children have different personalities. Most expectant parents don't spend much time thinking about personality. When the baby comes we kiss the baby's fuzzy head and never once imagine that one day you will fuss at him for drawing on the wall with crayons. However, if we reflect upon the reality that children really do have different personalities, it may help us understand our child's behavior. This does not erase our responsibility to teach and train our children, but it helps us understand that it will be harder for some children to respond positively to new people, or complete a task, or sit still in church.

> It may help to recognize that some of the traits you dislike in your child may actually serve them well as an adult.

It is normal for parents to wish their children were a little different, perhaps a little more outgoing, or less rambunctious. However, while temperament traits can be influenced, they will not be eliminated. Parents who struggle with certain traits of their children may do so because they are reminded of their own traits that they don't like and wish they could change. Or, they may be embarrassed by a behavior of their child that they think reflects badly on their parenting.

It may help to recognize that some of the traits you dislike in your child may actually serve them well as an adult. For example, intense children often become the adults who are passionate and creative. They may become leaders who make things happen. Children who are slow to warm up to new people or situations may become thoughtful, caring adults who empathize with others and become excellent counselors or caregivers.

Our son and our daughter were different in almost every way. I wish I had known that reality before we became parents. I think I would have spent less time trying to put him into her mold. Oh, we eventually came to celebrate the differences and now that they are adults we are equally proud of both of them. They are each making a positive but unique contribution to the world. I hope that after reading this chapter, you will be less inclined to compare your child with those of other couples, and less likely to compare your second child with your first.

Talking It Over

1. If you grew up with siblings, how are you different from each of your brothers and sisters?

2. Did your parents ever make statements of comparison between you and your siblings? If so, how did this make you feel?

3. As a child, did you ever compare yourself with your peers? If so, what were some of those comparisons? Did the comparisons help or hurt your self-esteem?

4. Were there certain foods that you disliked as a child? How did your parents respond to your unique tastes? Do you think their response was good for you?

5. Do you remember your parents ever talking about your sleep patterns when you were a young child?

6. What can you learn from how your parents did or did not compare you to other children?

7. How well do you feel you are prepared to accept your child as unique in the various areas we have discussed in this chapter?

8. Perhaps the two of you can discuss and agree that "we will accept our child as is, and not compare him/her with other children, nor try to impose our preconceived picture of the perfect child on him/her."

4

I Wish I'd Known . . .

That **POTTY TRAINING** *Is No Laughing Matter*

I must confess that before we became parents I never gave any thought to potty training. I knew that children did not stay in diapers forever, but I had no idea how or when they made the transition. However, once I changed a few diapers, I started asking my wife, "How long do we have to do this? When do babies learn to go to the potty? How do we teach them?" I was in for a rude awakening, as I discovered that potty training is no laughing matter.

I hope that this chapter will help you be better prepared than I was. Shannon and I recommend to our clients that they first prepare themselves for the process. An important first step is to acknowledge that your perspective and that of your child may be very different. Parents will likely see the process as desirable and rather easy. They say to their children, "You don't want to wear a wet dirty diaper now that you are a big boy, do you? You can do this, so let's try." The child, on the other hand, may feel confused or frightened with the idea of sitting on a toilet. Their thoughts may be: "You want me to do *what*? I'm really good at messing my diaper. Now, you want me to sit on that? I might fall in!"

By considering your child's perspective, you may be better able to approach the potty-training process with compassion and patience. Using the toilet certainly represents a major change for your child. Your ability to identify with his or her readiness to adjustment to change may make the training process more easily achievable for both of you.

One of the most common mistakes that parents make is to start potty training too early. In their eagerness to get out of the diaper stage, they push the child to do something he is not capable of doing. Again, as we learned in the last chapter, children are unique. Some are able to start potty training as early as eighteen months, others will not be ready until the age of three. So how do you know when to start training?

Are you ready?

First, observe your child. Here are some of the signs that a child is developmentally ready to begin training. One of the first is that they will begin to communicate that they have a messy diaper. They may point to their diaper or bring a new diaper to their parent. They may also express interest in using the bathroom because they have seen their parents or other siblings use it. They may ask questions, show interest in the tissue paper, or desire to flush the toilet. Parents might also suspect developmental readiness when the child's diaper is dry after taking a long morning or afternoon nap. These are some of the signs that a child is developmentally ready for potty training. If parents initiate efforts too early, the process will take longer and both parent and child will experience frustration.

Once you think your child is ready, the second question is, are *you* ready? Don't start the process when one of you has just taken a new job, or, when you have recently changed caregivers. If you are planning to move to another apartment or house in a few weeks, I suggest you delay potty training. Are you physically, emotionally, and mentally up to the task? Remember, this is no laughing matter. You may hear your friends say that they trained their child in one or two weeks. I would not count on that. You will have setbacks. It may take as much as three to five months before your child consistently controls his bladder and bowel movements. The younger the child is when you start training, the longer it may take to reach the goal. So get yourself ready for the marathon. If the race is shorter, then you can celebrate.

> The younger the child is when you start training, the longer it may take to reach the goal.

When both you and your child are ready to begin, one of the first steps is to purchase a potty chair or an adapter seat for your regular toilet. Most experts advise buying a child-sized potty, but the choice is yours. If you buy the adapter, make sure it feels comfortable and is attached firmly. You will also need to buy a stool to help the child get on and off the toilet, and to provide a platform for his feet so he can push during bowel movements.

Now that you have the equipment ready, how do you begin? I believe that books can be an easy and interesting way to pique the interest of your child. A number of good books are available:

Potty, It's Potty Time, "*Uh Oh! Gotta Go!*", *Everyone Poops,* and *Once Upon a Potty.* (You can easily locate these by Googling the titles.) Watching a video, such as Disney's *Nina Needs to Go,* is also an excellent way to stimulate conversation with your child. Resources such as these are written and illustrated in kid-friendly ways that both introduce children to the concept and encourage them in their efforts.

Now that the child is getting the idea, you can also stimulate their interest by allowing them to flush the toilet. Before a child will actually use the toilet, they seem to be interested in flushing. This experience expands the child's concept of the function of the toilet.

Time to sit!

At some point, the parents need to encourage the child to sit on the potty chair or on the toilet seat. Some pediatricians recommend starting with the child's clothes on. The purpose is to help the child feel comfortable sitting on the potty chair. Then move to sitting without a diaper or clothes. If you experience strong resistance, it is probably best to back off for a week or so and try again. A power struggle with your child will slow the process down.

Some parents use the child's favorite stuffed animal as an example. They may set the toy on a simulated potty chair while the child sits on the potty. Thus, the child and his/her toy animal are doing something together.

Buying your child "big boy" or "big girl" underwear may also be motivational for them. Small children's underwear is often decorated with cartoon characters with whom they are familiar. "You can wear this underwear when you learn to use the potty," can be an effective incentive for your child.

Establishing a routine where the child sits on the potty at certain times each day can help the child focus. Even if unsuccessful, the child is learning that going to the potty is a part of life. Some parents encourage their child to look at books while on the toilet. I suggest that this may be most helpful if the books are on the topic of "using the potty."

If after sitting on the potty with the diaper off, the child still is not successful, some parents have found that if they take the diaper off and let the child play without it, the child will go to the potty when the bladder is full. Once they are successful, you have crossed a significant milepost. The second milepost is a bowel movement in the potty. When this happens, you are on the road to success. However, don't expect perfection. Being "on the road" is not the same as crossing the finish line. There will be mistakes and messes to clean up, but day by day, week by week, and sometimes month by month, your child's success rate will improve.

During the night

Once daytime control is in place, it's time to think about nighttime control. I don't want to discourage you, but this may take even more time. It all depends on how soundly your child sleeps and how well his/her bladder can hold the urine. You may want to try a few nights without diapers (be sure and protect your mattress). If the child is not successful, then return to the diapers. Communicate to your child that he/she is not quite ready, but we will try again in a month or so.

One step that may be helpful is to request that the child use the bathroom just before going to bed. Another is restricting what he drinks before bedtime. However, if your child is not successful immediately, don't panic. Pediatricians indicate that some children will have nighttime accidents for several months and sometimes years. I know you are hoping your child does not fall into this category, but it is not abnormal.

Healthy attitudes and best practices

Shannon and I would like to recommend the following attitudes and practices as you face the challenge of potty training your child. It is no laughing matter, but we believe the following ideas will help you be successful. I wish I had known these things before Karolyn and I became parents.

Maintain healthy expectations. Remember every child is unique. Don't force your child to remain on the potty. In your frustration, you may feel the need to do so, but force actually can slow the process. If your frustration level becomes such that you feel the need to force your child or threaten him or her with lost privileges or punishment if he or she does not use the potty, then you need to consider taking a "time-out" for yourself to regain composure and perspective. Have no fear, children will eventually learn to use the potty. Healthy expectations by parents can have many positive outcomes for them, and their children.

Have fun. Maintaining a fun attitude whenever possible can help keep the training process positive. Some parents attempt to keep it fun by using toilet training songs. For example, set to the tune of "The Wheels on the Bus Go Round and Round," you can sing something like: "This is the way we pee in the potty, pee in the potty, pee in the potty. This is the way we pee in the potty. All day long." The tunes of any number of childhood songs lend themselves to being playfully rewritten for training purposes. Fun tactics such as this can help remove much of your child's anxiety.

Reward appropriately. Even the simplest reward may be worthwhile incentive for your child to keep up his/her efforts. A special sticker, three M&M'S, or anything that your child likes will motivate. Many reward possibilities exist, so much so that parents need only to think through their preferences about what is practical, affordable, and sensible. Small rewards can be given even if the child only tries and does not actually succeed. One warning: don't go overboard with rewards. Large candy bars or expensive toys will send the wrong message. Children may use this against you when they get a little older. It's called manipulating parents. "I'll do this, but only if you get me a new bicycle."

Expect failure. Remember, this is no laughing matter. Children may fail many times in their efforts before finally succeeding. Expecting some failure will aid you in your efforts. Expect: wetting and soiling trial underwear and accidents in the floor at home and in public places. By expecting these and other potential failures, parents will approach training with more realism and save themselves and their children unnecessary frustration.

Be ready when they are ready, especially when you are in public places. Shannon shares her experience. "Stephen and I are amazed that our children want to go to the bathroom just as we receive our order at the restaurant or just as we drive onto the highway. Similarly, they have an uncanny ability to need to go and go multiple times during a concert or sporting event, and just when our favorite song or an important moment in the game takes place." Yes, if your child is ready to go, then you must be ready to go.

Just a word about public restrooms. When you are in the process of training your child, you cannot "hole up" in your house forever. Don't let training keep you from traveling or going out to eat. Prepare for the event. Take your potty chair or toilet adapter.

Flushable potty seat covers and hand sanitizer are also important. I know you are conscientious about your child's health, but as time goes on, you will be able to overcome your germ phobias and come to appreciate the convenience of public restrooms.

Be patient. Sooner or later, your child will be able to use the bathroom on his/her own. I know that in rare cases, there are medical problems and physical disabilities that may prevent this. These parents will need to rely on medical authorities to help their child reach his or her potential in this area.

More common, but still challenging, is the reality that some children may experience nighttime bed-wetting challenges that may or may not be due to medical conditions. This problem may persist even into the teenage years. For these children, who are otherwise trained, parents may consider using absorbent underwear made especially for children who struggle with this problem. Parents facing this issue will want to consult appropriate resources, including their child's pediatrician, and websites from such companies as GoodNites, which is one of many brands of products made to assist children with nighttime bed-wetting problems. No matter the cause or duration of a child's nighttime bed-wetting, parents' balance between being patient with the problem and treating the problem will be helpful to both the parents and their children in the long run.

> Look for even the smallest successes along the way and celebrate them.

Celebrate successes. Don't wait until the final goal is accomplished. Look for even the smallest successes along the way and celebrate them. High fives, hugs, happy dances, and anything else that communicates how proud you are of the child's success are ways of celebrating. After all, the work that you and your child have put into this training is deserving of celebration!

When you and your children will have long forgotten their potty-training days, this experience will have served as one of yours and their first major, collaborative problem-solving efforts. As challenging as this training may have been, you will have modeled many virtues for your child such as: patience, diligence, encouragement, hope, and the joy of succeeding. The practice you and your child received will carry over into other problem-solving opportunities that will arise throughout childhood.

Remember this: millions of parents have lived through the process of potty training, and so will you. After all, you too went through this experience as a child, and now, as an adult, my guess is that you don't remember much about it. Ask your parents; they too may have few memories. So take heart. You are up to the task. After reading this chapter, you may even find yourself laughing when you experience some of the things we have discussed.

Talking It Over

I know that before your child is born, you are probably not thinking about potty training. But when the time comes, here are some additional things you may want to do.

1. Read this chapter again and underline the practical ideas we have shared.

2. Talk with your parents about what they remember when you were in the process of potty training. What techniques did they use? How long did it take?

3. Talk with a couple that has been successful in potty training

their child. What techniques did they use? How long did it take? (Remember no two children are alike.)

4. Go online and read some of the articles on potty training.

5. Discuss with your spouse the pros and cons of potty chairs versus adaptable toilet seats.

6. Practice singing the following words to the tune of "The Wheels on the Bus Go Round and Round." "This is the way we pee in the potty, pee in the potty, pee in the potty. This is the way we pee in the potty. All day long." (Sing it with your spouse if you want a good laugh.) Someday, you will find the appropriate time to sing it with your child.

7. Keep a positive attitude and remember, sooner or later, your child will learn to use the toilet.

I Wish I'd Known . . .

That Children Need BOUNDARIES

I think I knew, in a general sense, that parents were responsible for establishing rules to protect and guide their child to maturity. I just did not know how soon the process would begin and how long it would last. I discovered that it is an eighteen-year job, and that the first ten years are the most important. In fact, the degree to which you help your child live within healthy boundaries by the age of ten will largely determine the quality of the relationship you have with your teenager.

Healthy boundaries grow out of concern for the well-being of the child. They are not arbitrary rules passed down from generation to generation. We want our children to be safe, healthy, and good decision makers. Eventually, we hope they will become responsible, self-controlled adults who will make a positive impact on the world.

> The degree to which you help your child live within healthy boundaries by the age of ten will largely determine the quality of the relationship you have with your teenager.

But the challenges of helping children walk this path change from year to year as the culture changes. In fact, the culture itself imposes new rules for child safety from time to time. Shannon reminded me that you will face the reality of boundaries the moment you leave the hospital with your newborn and need to properly seat belt them in their specially designed car seat.

Where it all begins

In this country, parents of infants who deliver their babies in hospitals must show evidence to a nurse or other staff member that they have a proper car seat and that their baby is properly secured in that seat before leaving the hospital. Federal law (National Highway Traffic Safety Administration) requires that children traveling in motor vehicles be properly restrained in car seats until an age at which they are big enough to fit in a regular seat with seat belt properly fastened. There was no such law when our first child was born. However, such laws are based on the hard, cold facts related to child safety in today's world.

Your infant will not likely resist your efforts to put them in the car seat as you drive home from the hospital (though they may cry for a few minutes). However, I can assure you that as they get a bit older, they will not always want to be strapped in their car seat. As a toddler, they are developmentally more interested in exerting their will and their desire for freedom than complying with your rules. Parents are now faced with having to enforce car-seat safety with children who don't understand or care about car-seat safety. So what's a parent to do?

You must discipline yourself to enforce the boundary placed on you by the laws of the land, because you know it is for the safety of your child. Shannon told me two of her favorite statements: "I can put you in your seat, or you can get into it by yourself." Or, "Can you get in your seat by the time I count to five? One . . . two . . . three . . . " Age-appropriate tactics like these allow a child the opportunity to be a part of the decision. In this case, both the parents and the child "win."

Of course, ultimately, the child must get in the car seat. So, if persuasion fails, parents must carefully and lovingly exert their physical size and strength to help the child into the seat. However, this must be done lovingly and not in anger. In anger, some parents may unintentionally physically hurt their child while getting them into the seat.

Cheer up! By age four, children are typically developmentally able to get in the car seat and safely buckle and unbuckle their seat belts with little or no assistance from their parents. Parents may welcome this convenience, but with their child's increased independence comes a new inconvenience—the child's ability to unbuckle his or her seat belt without permission. Shannon says about her own experience, "We have had to stop the car numerous times to remind one of the children that we cannot continue until they attach their seat belt. This normally works well, especially if we are on the way to get ice cream. Of course, if it doesn't work, we are back to exerting parental authority (hopefully in a loving, kind manner)."

Why have I taken so much time to talk about car seats? Because that is where it all begins—on that first day that you take your baby for a car ride. This is the first time your child is

> When I studied cultural anthropology, I discovered that there are no cultures that do not have a moral code.

experiencing the benefits of boundary setting as it relates to safety and compliance with laws. The compliance with cultural laws (or rules) is important if a child is to grow to be a responsible citizen.

Before I studied counseling, I did an undergraduate and graduate degree in cultural anthropology. I discovered that there are no cultures that do not have a moral code. There are things that children do and don't do in every culture. The same is true of adults. Parents play the most important role in teaching the child generally accepted standards of conduct.

Babies are not capable of deciding how to live, and without parental rules, a child will not survive to adulthood. During infancy, parents must totally enforce the rules and control the behavior of the child. This means that they will not allow Johnny to crawl into a fire, no matter how attracted he may be to the rising flames. Later, as a toddler, Johnny must be kept out of the street lest he be hit by a passing car. His parents must put medicines and toxic substances out of his reach.

The reality of rules

From this infantile stage requiring total control, parents move toward helping their child to develop self-discipline. This road to maturity is one that every child must walk and for which every parent needs to accept responsibility. It is an awesome task, requiring wisdom, imagination, patience, and great amounts of love. It is my desire that this chapter will help you be better prepared for the task than I was when our first child was born.

Let's begin with one simple reality: parents are older than children! With increased age, we assume they have more wisdom than children. Thus, parents are to make the rules they believe are best for the child. Today's busy, tired parents often find it easier to let little Jacob or Emma stay up late or eat junk food. It is true that some parents abuse their authority. However, the greater danger is to rear a child who grows up without the limits they so desperately need. In a healthy and loving family, parental authority is used for the benefit of the children. The parents are committed to high ethical and moral standards. They espouse the virtues of kindness, love, honesty, forgiveness, integrity, hard work, and treating others with respect. Children who obey such parents will reap the benefit of living under wholesome authority.

However, before we talk about how to make healthy rules, I want to address one other important issue. Parents must distinguish between what is developmentally appropriate behavior and what is misbehavior. Developmentally appropriate behavior is that in which a child is exploring and discovering how the world around him or her works. That may mean a one-year-old child makes a mess while playing with his or her food, a two-year-old child says no to many requests because he or she is learning to talk, or a three-year-old splashes in the bathtub because it is fun to splash. Older children might do things like use household items to build a fort in their bedroom, accidentally mark on a table while drawing or painting, or unintentionally scratch their parents' car while riding their bike a little too close to the car.

Any of these behaviors may upset a parent, and certainly instances like these are teaching opportunities for parents to share what is or is not acceptable. However, these types of behavior are not true misbehavior. They are developmentally expected

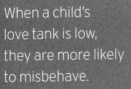

When a child's love tank is low, they are more likely to misbehave.

behavior. Children are exploring and discovering their surroundings. They are having fun. They are growing in their physical and cognitive abilities such that they are increasingly less clumsy and more able to learn and follow rules and expectations. Because of these developmental realities, parents are wise to be patient and first consider the developmental aspects of children's behaviors before immediately considering such behaviors as misbehavior.

Over time, as parents continue to teach their children about rules and expectations, and as children become better able to understand right from wrong behavior, parents can have greater confidence in distinguishing between behavior and misbehavior.

True misbehavior, when a child willfully breaks a rule, must be examined. A good question to ask is, "Why would my child do that?" Alfred Adler, a well-known, pioneering psychotherapist, suggested four possibilities: attention, power, revenge, and inadequacy. I would add: the need for love. When a child's love tank is low, they are more likely to misbehave. If you understand what is behind the misbehavior, you are more likely to have a positive response.

Adler suggested that if you look at your own emotional response to the child's misbehavior, you will likely be able to determine what is going on inside the child. If the behavior is motivated by the need for attention, you may find yourself annoyed. If power is behind the behavior, you will likely become angry and go into power-struggle mode. If revenge, you will feel hurt and perhaps shame the child. If inadequacy is behind the behavior, you may feel helpless and emotionally disconnected. By being more in touch with your own feelings, you may better understand your child's misbehavior and respond in more effective ways than coaxing, overpowering, shaming, or shunning your child.[1]

Now let's turn our attention to the task of setting healthy boundaries. Boundaries are rules set by parents for the whole-some development of the child. The establishment of boundaries must be coupled with the concept of consequences when bound-aries are ignored. Children need to learn that all behavior will have consequences. Obedient behavior brings positive consequences; disobedient behavior brings negative consequences. This pro-cess involves three things: setting rules, setting consequences (good as well as bad), and administering discipline. Let's examine these three.

Setting rules

To do or not to do, that is the nature of rules. Rules give guide-lines for family living. These are things we do not do in our family: chew gum at the table, bounce a basketball in the kitchen, leave the house with candles burning, jump on the sofa, or mistreat the dog. These are things we do in our family: put tools away when we have finished using them, put toys away when we have finished playing with them, turn lights off when we leave the room, throw our dirty clothes in the laundry room, and say "May I be excused" when we leave the dinner table. All families have rules, but not all families have healthy rules.

Good rules have four characteristics: they are *intentional*, they are *mutual*, they are *reasonable*, and they are *discussed* with the entire family. Intentional rules are those to which we have given conscious thought. They do not simply emerge from our own frustration at the moment, but they have come with considerable thought as to why the rule is needed, what is its purpose, and whether it is really for the benefit of everyone.

Intentional rules mean that we don't have a rule simply because it was a rule in our own families. For example, we once had a rule that "we don't sing at the table." One day, Karolyn asked me why we had that rule. I said, "Well, that was a rule at my house." Karolyn replied, "I know it was also a rule at my house, but what's wrong with singing at the table. It is a way of expressing joy. I want the kids to have positive memories around the table." I could not think of a good answer, so we dropped that rule.

Second, good rules involve mutual input from the father and the mother. Each of us grew up in different families; consequently, we had different rules. I tend to bring my rules to the marriage and my wife brings her rules. If these rules do not agree, we often have conflicts over the rules. These conflicts should be resolved by listening to each other, treating the other person with respect, and looking for a solution on which both of us can agree. For example, if you believe that children's intentional burping is utterly uncivilized and your husband thinks it's cute, perhaps you can disallow it in the house and the car but permit it in the backyard. When parents disagree on the rules and argue in front of the child, the child is confused and will eventually join in the argument.

Healthy rules are also reasonable. They serve some positive function. The overarching questions are: "Is this rule good for the child? Will it have some positive effect on the child's life?" Here are some practical questions to ask as you decide about a particular rule.

Does this rule keep the child from danger?

Does this rule teach the child some positive character trait:

honesty, hard work, kindness, sharing, etc.?

Does this rule protect property?

Does this rule teach the child responsibility?

Does this rule teach good manners?

These are the factors that concern us as parents. We want to keep our children from danger. We do not want our young child to be hit by a car, and we do not want our older children to get involved in drugs. We want to teach our children positive character traits in keeping with our values. We want children to respect the property of others; thus, a rule about not playing baseball in the backyard may well keep them from breaking a neighbor's window. We want them to learn to take care of their own possessions; thus, the rule about putting the bicycle in the storage shed at night is a purposeful rule.

Healthy rules are also clearly explained to the entire family. Unspoken rules are unfair rules. A child cannot be expected to live up to a standard of which he is unaware. Parents have the responsibility for making sure that children understand what the rules are. As children grow older, they need to know why their parents have decided on this rule.

In making family rules, it is perfectly legitimate to consult other parents, schoolteachers, and extended family, and to read books and magazine articles. To have the best possible rules, parents need all the wisdom they can get.

Setting consequences

The sign by the side of the road read: "$250 fine for speeding." I lifted my foot off the accelerator. I did not have $250 that I wanted to give away. The breaking of civil rules usually brings negative consequences. One of the difficulties of our society is that in recent years, the consequences of wrongdoing have been delayed by long and tedious court procedures, and on many occasions the consequences have been minimal. I believe that this has contributed to the growth of civil misconduct over the last several decades. Effective motivation to civil obedience requires quick and certain consequences.

In the family, the principle is the same. Obedience is learned by suffering the consequences of disobedience. Effective teaching of obedience requires that consequences for breaking rules should cause discomfort to the rule breaker.

There are two types of consequences: natural and logical. Natural consequences are those that come about without the parent having to do much of anything. For example, if a child refuses to eat what his parents have prepared for dinner, then he will naturally get hungry (natural consequence). Parents can allow this hunger because they know that sooner or later, the child will ask to eat. They can then remind the child that they are hungry because they did not eat dinner, and inform them that we will have breakfast in the morning. If you think this is cruel, then you can give them a snack and inform them that the next time they do not eat dinner the snack will be smaller. Missing a meal will not harm a child, but it will teach them that dinner is the time to eat in our house. The parents do not have to coax, overpower, shame, or shun their child for not eating; they can simply allow the refusal to eat, acknowledge the child's choice, and then wait for the teaching moment, or moments, that will follow.

In other instances, logical consequences may be the better choice. The consequence has a logical connection to the broken rule. For example, a child may be careless with his electronic device or other toy. The rule is to put it back "in its place" when you finish playing. If not, the child loses the privilege of playing with it the next day. If he breaks the rule, the loss of privilege may be frustrating enough to the child that he will learn to take care of his possessions.

I highly recommend that you determine the consequences when you make the rule and inform the child of both the rule and the consequences of breaking the rule. For example, the rule is that we do not throw the ball inside the house. If you do, the consequence is that the ball goes in the trunk of the car for two days, and if you break something, you will need to pay for it out of your allowance. The rule is clear and the consequences are clear. Everyone has this information. Now, if the child breaks the rule, mom and dad both know what to do, and the child knows what to expect. Parents are less likely to overreact by yelling and screaming at the child, and more likely to kindly administer the consequences. Which brings us to the third characteristic of healthy boundaries.

Kindly but firmly administer the consequences

The key word here is consistency. If we apply the discipline one day and let the offense slide the next day, the child is confused. He is asking, "Is this a rule or not? Are there consequences or not?" As parents we must not allow our own emotional state to determine how and when we discipline the child. This is why setting the logical consequences before the infraction occurs is so important. You don't have to think "What shall I do now?" You already know what to do; it is just a matter of doing it with kindness and firmness.

> If we apply the discipline one day and let the offense slide the next day, the child is confused.

In our book *The 5 Love Languages of Children*,[2] Dr. Ross Campbell and I encourage couples to "wrap" their discipline in love. That is, when you are ready to administer the consequences, you speak the child's primary love language before and after the discipline. For example, if the child's love language is words of affirmation, and they break the rule about throwing the ball in the house, you might say, "Mark, I want you to know how proud I am of you. You seldom break the rules and that is good. But, you know that you broke the rule about throwing the ball in the house, so you know what has to happen, right?" Mark is likely to say, "Yes, I'm sorry. I forgot." The parent says, "I can understand that but the ball must go in the trunk of the car for two days. I'm just glad that nothing was broken. I'm so proud of you. Most of the time you keep the rules. I love you so much." Mark hands over the ball feeling sad, but loved, and he has learned that breaking the rules always has consequences.

I cannot overstate the value of setting clear boundaries for your child, not only for the child's safety but for building the child's self-worth, character, and decision-making skills. Too many parents allow children to push down their boundaries with little or no resistance. Moms and dads are often so tired from the daily grind that when a child resists a boundary, the parent reasons, "It's not worth the hassle," so they cave in and the child does what he wishes.

Every time a boundary falls, the child feels less secure. The child pushes subconsciously hoping that the wall is firm. When the wall falls, the child's world is more confusing. One fifteen-year-old young man said in my office, "Is there anyone who stands for anything anymore? Everyone seems to accept anything, given the right situation. I wish adults gave us more guidance. Haven't they learned something during their life that would help us avoid some mistakes?" This young man realized the importance of boundaries even if his parents did not.

I hope that this chapter will help you set healthy boundaries for your child. Few things are more important in your role as a parent.

Talking It Over

1. If you are waiting for your child to be born, it is time to purchase the car seat, which you will need when you take your baby home from the hospital. Or, select the seat that you would like and give the information to someone who would like to give you a nice and necessary gift.

2. With your spouse, make a list of the rules you remember from your childhood. Discuss which of these rules you plan to have for your child.

3. Are there other rules that you think will be important in rearing your child?

4. Discuss with your spouse what might be logical consequences if your child breaks each of these rules.

5. When you were a child, did your parents discuss with you the consequences if you broke the rules? If not, how do you remember your parents' response when you broke a rule?

6. Did you ever feel that your parents were being unfair in their discipline? If so, what was it that you felt was unfair?

7. Look around your house or apartment and ask each other, "What are some of the things we will need to do to protect our young child from getting hurt?"

8. As an adult, do you see yourself as a rule keeper or a rule breaker? How do you think your model will influence your child?

I Wish I'd Known . . .

That Children's
EMOTIONAL HEALTH
Is as Important as
PHYSICAL HEALTH

Both of our children were born before I became a counselor. I had studied anthropology, sociology, Greek, Hebrew, and theology, but I knew very little about emotions. Of course, I knew that sometimes I felt loved, sad, happy, angry, frustrated, and discouraged, but I attributed those to the behavior of my wife. When she was kind and loving to me, life was beautiful. When she treated me harshly, I felt rejected, hurt, and a whole other bundle of negative emotions. I had no idea how to handle these emotions, so we had some rocky years before we learned how to listen, affirm each other, and look for solutions rather than arguing.

However, that was a situation of two adults trying to "get it together." The whole idea of children and their emotional needs was not even on my radar. Years later, I studied child development, and a whole new world of insight opened to me. I came to understand my own childhood better. I realized that I played a significant role in the emotional development of our children. So, in this chapter, I want to share with you some of the things I wish I'd known about the emotional health of children.

> Emotional health and physical health are the two tracks on which the train of parenting must run.

Parents are naturally concerned about their child's physical health. Thus, they make regular pediatric visits to their medical doctor. They will call the nurse if the child seems to have some physical reactions that they do not understand. If they awaken during the night, they will check the crib to make sure the baby is breathing. All of this grows out of parental concern for the physical well-being of their child. Such concern is wise, natural, and necessary. Keeping the child alive and healthy is a prerequisite to everything else.

However, assuming the child is alive and healthy, our next major concern should be for the emotional health of the child. Emotional health and physical health are the two tracks on which the train of parenting must run. Both are necessary if we are to raise a healthy, responsible child. Some parents give little thought to the child's emotional needs. Their attitude is "I love my child and I'm doing everything I can to keep them healthy and growing. So I hope they turn out okay." Hoping and trusting, however, are not enough; parents must be proactive to ensure their child's emotional health. So, what are the emotional needs of a child?

If you have taken a basic psychology course, you may be

familiar with John Bowlby's attachment theory,[1] and Erik Erikson's psychosocial stages of development.[2] When Shannon and I were discussing this chapter, she reminded me of these significant studies. These well-known psychological models provide important insight for parents who wish to take proactive steps in nurturing their children's emotional health. So let me share each of these briefly.

The importance of attachment

Attachment is an emotional bond of trust shared between people who care deeply for one another. (Hopefully you have this kind of emotional bond with your spouse.) What we now know is that children who do not develop this emotional bond with their parents or other caregivers will have difficulty developing such a bond in adulthood. According to Bowlby, parents enhance attachment by being available and responsive to their infants' emotional and physical needs. Infants, in turn, are comforted by and learn to trust their parents' presence and care. They then develop a sense of security because of the emotional bond that exists between them. Early attachment theorists thought that simply providing an infant with food was the key to building this attachment. However, over time, attachment theorists discovered that it was parents' emotional nurturance of their children, by such things as cuddling, talking, singing, and otherwise creating a safe and positive environment, that more heavily influence the child's successful attachment to the parents.

With this kind of nurture, children develop a healthy sense of security that enables them to confidently explore the world around them. It is also their initial bond with their parents that enables them to bond to others as they grow older. Thus, parents' emotional and relational closeness and care in their children's early years serves as a template that will guide their children's trust of and emotional engagement in relationships across time. This is an extremely important insight for parents. This is why parents need to spend as much time as possible bonding with their young children in a loving, kind, supportive environment.

Stages of emotional development

Erik Erikson, a contemporary of Bowlby, saw this bonding as so important that he listed "trust versus mistrust" as the first stage of his eight-stage psychosocial model. He indicated that this first stage occurs between birth and one and a half years old. Infants experience uncertainty of various types during this time, and this uncertainty is alleviated through the dependable, loving care of their parents. As a result of their parents' consistency and emotional warmth, the infant's fear is replaced with hope that their needs will be met. This sense of hopefulness adds to a healthy sense of security that will influence all other aspects of their lives.

"Autonomy versus shame," the second stage of Erikson's psychosocial model, marks the period from ages one and a half years old to three years old. At these ages, children are becoming increasingly more curious about the world around them and equally more able to explore that world. Parents who encourage and allow safe exploration enable their children to experience age-appropriate freedom, which results in feelings of self-confidence and self-worth for the child. Believing that they can succeed in life and that they are worthwhile individuals will positively influence children their entire lives. Likewise, if they are not allowed healthy autonomy and the chance to learn from failures, children may feel self-doubt and shame and generally feel that they are unable to succeed in life. Parents are wise to encourage and enable their children's healthy, age-appropriate independence. In so doing they help their children gain a healthy sense of autonomy.

"Initiative versus guilt," Erikson's third stage, occurs between ages three to five years old. During this stage, children are more interested in engaging other children in play. They are also more inquisitive. They want to make some choices for themselves. Thus, at this age, children take more initiative. If appropriately encouraged by their parents, children will experience an increased sense of self-worth and purpose. If not appropriately encouraged, or if unnecessarily discouraged, or prevented by parents from taking reasonable initiative, children will feel that their actions are unworthy or wrong. They may experience guilt growing out of their parents' discouragement or criticism. Of course, children, like adults, are wrong from time to time, but this gives the parents an opportunity to acknowledge any right intention that the child had and to teach the child about right ways of taking initiative. One way to encourage initiative is to give the child a choice between two equally positive decisions. The parent may say, "Would you like to bring your tricycle inside before dinner or after dinner?" Either way, the child gets to show initiative. Children learn to make decisions by making decisions.

The fourth stage of psychosocial development occurs between five and twelve years of age. It is "competence versus inferiority." Building on the initiative they hopefully achieved in the previous stage, children now are rapidly growing in knowledge, ability and desire to succeed in their undertakings. They want to feel competent, and they want to feel that they are accepted by their peer group. Also, during this stage, children want to gain the approval of their parents, teachers, and coaches.

Parents, peers, teachers, and coaches all can help encourage children to reach their potential. If supported and encouraged, children will develop a sense of competence and belief in themselves that they can reach goals and excel. If not supported and encouraged, or if unnecessarily criticized or prevented from reaching reasonable goals, children may develop a sense of inferiority or poor self-esteem.

When affirming a child, focus on effort, not perfection. If a five-year-old makes his own bed, you might say, "I can see that you worked hard on this. I really appreciate your effort." Later that day, you might say, "Let me show you one thing when you make your bed in the morning." Then you give a tip. The child will likely take the tip because they felt affirmed. If a ten-year-old mows the grass, don't say, "You didn't get under the bushes. Can't you see this grass under the bushes?" Rather, you affirm them for the grass they cut. "Thanks for your hard work on the yard. I really appreciate what you did." Next Saturday, before they mow again, you explain how to get the grass under the bushes. "See this grass under the bushes. It is hard to get. You have to move the mower in and out, but I know you can do it." You bet they will. Affirmation helps a child develop confidence.

I will not deal with the other stages that Erikson discusses because they are beyond the scope of this book, but hopefully you are beginning to see the importance of helping your child develop emotional health as they grow physically. In summary, four areas in which a child needs to develop emotional health are:

- attachment, not neglect
- autonomy, not shame

- initiative, not guilt
- confidence, not inferiority

I am not suggesting that physical needs are not important. They are! Without food, shelter, air, water, warmth, and sleep, the child will not survive. Also, the child's safety is important. We discussed the importance of boundaries in the last chapter. However, while we are meeting these needs, we must not neglect the child's emotional development. Parents have the greatest degree of influence on their child's emotional development.

When parents love and care for their children, their children are in turn more likely to be able to fully love and care for themselves and others. Parents may instinctively know this to be true. Healthy parents also may instinctively desire to love and care for their children as infants. However, as children age out of the infant stage, become more independent, and exhibit more individuality, parents may make less intentional effort to express love and to build the relationship with their children. Parents may get busy with other responsibilities and find it easy to take for granted that the children are okay as long as they are physically healthy. Yet children may be physically strong but emotionally challenged. We all know healthy adults who live with feelings of inferiority, anger, guilt, shame, and loneliness. They are physically healthy but emotionally challenged. This lack of emotional health will likely hamper their success in relationships and vocations. As parents, this is not what we want for our children. Thus, we must be proactive in seeking to meet emotional needs.

> We all know adults who are physically healthy but emotionally challenged.

Your child's love tank

In walking with your child through these developmental stages, I believe that the deepest emotional need a child has is the need to feel loved by parents. Feeling loved is the essential ingredient in forming that emotional bond between child and parent. It is also the foundation for encouraging the child's autonomy, initiative, and confidence. I like to picture inside every child an emotional love tank. When the love tank is full, that is, the child genuinely feels loved by the parents, they tend to grow up to become secure, loving adults who can build healthy relationships and accomplish their goals. When a child does not feel loved by parents, they tend to grow up with many internal emotional struggles, and in the teen years, they often go looking for love in all the wrong places.

Most parents love their children, but not all children feel loved. It is not enough to be sincere; we must make sure we are emotionally connecting with the child. Years ago, I discovered that there are fundamentally five ways that children receive love. I call them the five love languages. Out of the five, each child has a primary love language. That is, one language speaks more deeply emotionally than the other four. If you don't speak their primary love language, they will not feel loved even though you are expressing love in some of the other languages.

> Most parents love their children, but not all children feel loved.

This explains why a thirteen-year-old will sit in my office and say, "My parents don't love me. They love my brother, but they don't love me." I know his parents and I know that they love him, and they would be shocked if they heard what I am hearing. The problem is they never learned his primary love language. So let me briefly review these five languages and share how you can discover your child's primary love language.

Words of Affirmation

There is an ancient Hebrew proverb that says, "Life and death are in the power of the tongue." That is certainly true in the way you speak to a child. Harsh, critical words kill the child's confidence and create fear and anger. Positive encouraging words instill courage and security. "I like your beautiful red hair. Your arm muscles are getting strong. I really appreciate your helping me with the dishes. Thanks for the way you shared your toys with Tommy," are all words of affirmation.

For the infant, it is the tone of voice and not the words themselves that positively impact the baby's emotional health. With a warm, fun voice, you can say, "You are the sweetest baby in the world. Yes, you are." Or, you can say, "You are the meanest baby in the world. Yes, you are." The infant does not understand the words but is affirmed by the tone of voice. But in a few months the words themselves, along with the tone of voice, become extremely important.

Quality Time

Quality time is giving your child your undivided attention. You may be playing a game, working on a project, or having a conversation. The important factor is that your attention is focused on the child. Sending a text message while talking with your child is not quality time, unless you are teaching him how to send a text message.

Gifts

In my anthropology studies, I discovered that giving gifts is a universal language of love. The gift communicates, "I was thinking about you. I thought you might like this. I love you." The gift need not be expensive. It truly is "the thought that counts." I like to remind parents that a gift should not be attached to demands or expectations. When you say, "I will give you this candy if you will clean up your room," the candy is no longer a gift but payment for services rendered. I'm not saying you shouldn't pay your child for work. I'm simply saying that such payment is not a gift. The word *gift* comes from the Greek word *grace*, which means unmerited favor.

As parents we are responsible gift givers. We don't give children anything that we think would be detrimental to them. No, you don't have to get your child a phone because "everyone else has one." As parents, we must use good judgment in what we give our children. When you yield to a child's temper tantrums and give them what they are demanding, you are the one who is now being manipulated.

Acts of Service

"Actions speak louder than words." You have heard that old saying. For some children this is true. When the child is born and for several months thereafter, you are forced to speak this language to your child. An infant is helpless. You must put the food in and take the food out. They cannot care for themselves. As they get older this language is spoken by mending doll dresses, fixing tricycles, pumping up the football, etc. As they get even older, you speak this language by teaching them to do things for themselves. It takes much more effort to teach a child how to cook than it does to cook for them, but this skill will greatly enhance their future.

Physical Touch

We have long known the emotional power of physical touch. That is why we pick up babies and cuddle them in our arms and say all those silly things to them. Long before they understand the meaning of the word love, they feel loved by tender physical touch. All the research agrees that babies who are held, caressed, and kissed develop a healthier emotional life than those who are left for long periods of time without physical contact.

As the infant becomes a toddler and the toddler reaches school age, the need for physical touch does not diminish. All children need affirming touch, but for some, this is love's loudest voice. Without affirming touch, their emotional health will be negatively affected.

As noted above, out of these five love languages, each child has a primary love language. One language will speak more deeply emotionally than the other four. If a child does not receive heavy doses of his/her primary language, they will not feel loved even though the parent is speaking some of the other love languages.

> All children need affirming touch, but for some, this is love's loudest voice.

Discovering your child's love language

So, how do you discover a child's primary love language?

Observe the child's behavior

Observe how the child consistently engages parents and

others. If they are always wanting to help you do things, their language is likely acts of service. If they often make gifts for you and others, then gifts may be their language. My son's language is physical touch. I discovered it when he was three or four years old. When I came home in the afternoon, he would run to the door and grab my leg and want me to pick him up. If I sat down, he was all over me. He was touching me because he wanted to be touched.

My daughter never did that. She would say, "Daddy, come into my room, I want to show you something." She wanted my undivided attention—quality time. If your child often says, "Thanks, Mommy" or, "You did a good job, Mommy," then you may assume that words of affirmation is his/her love language.

What do they complain about?

One four-year-old said to his mother, "We don't ever go to the park together since the baby came." He is complaining about the lack of quality time. Another child said to his mother, "Dad doesn't care that my bicycle is broken." His complaint calls for acts of service. The complaint often reveals the primary love language.

What do they request most often?

The child who asks you to play with them or read a story to them is requesting quality time. The child who asks for a back rub is requesting physical touch. If your child constantly solicits comments on his work, then his love language may be words of affirmation. Questions such as, "Mom, what do you think of the paper I wrote?" or "Does this outfit look okay?" or "Dad, how did I do in the game?" are all requests for words of affirmation.

If you put these three together: observe how they love others, listen to their complaints and requests, you will likely be able to discover your child's primary love language.

Please do not hear me saying that you only speak the child's primary love language. What I am suggesting is that you regularly and often speak the primary language, but you also sprinkle in the other four. We want our children to learn how to give and receive love in all five languages. This produces emotional health. This also best prepares the child for healthy adult relationships.

As a parent, you may not have learned how to give and receive love in some of these languages. So, if you did not receive words of affirmation as a child, you may find it hard to express such words to your children. The good news is that all of these languages can be learned as adults. Don't let your own childhood keep you from meeting the emotional needs of your children. (For additional help see *The 5 Love Languages of Children*, which I wrote with psychiatrist, Dr. Ross Campbell.[3] Or visit *www.5lovelanguages.com.*)

For those parents who were severely abused or traumatized as a child and, as a result, may feel emotionally unhealthy or lack confidence in their parenting, I would highly recommend counseling. The hurt, anger, fear, depression, and other emotions will not go away with the passing of time. I would also recommend finding churches or other organizations in your community that offer support groups. By reaching out for help, you can begin the journey of becoming emotionally healthy. Your child deserves your best efforts.

In some cases, parents and children will share the same love language, and parents will need only to remember to actually speak their own language to the child. Other parents who do not share the same love language as their children will need to be even more intentional in learning to speak the child's love language. As with learning an actual spoken language, learning a new love language will take effort. However, in time, it will become easier and feel more natural to you. The reward is in seeing your child flourish emotionally. I assure you, the reward is worth the effort.

I wish I had known the things I have shared in this chapter before we became parents. I hope that these concepts will help you rear an emotionally healthy child.

Talking It Over

1. In your early childhood, do you feel that the emotional bond between you and your mother was deep and abiding? What about the emotional bond with your father? How do you think this has affected you as an adult?

2. How do you think you will be different from your parents in bonding with your child?

3. On a scale of 0 to 10 how would you rank your own level of self-confidence? What do you think contributed to this?

4. On a scale of 0 to 10 how much guilt, shame, and feelings of inferiority did you feel during your teen years? What do you think contributed to this?

5. On a scale of 0 to 10 how much love did you feel from your mother and father as you grew up? Why?

6. How much love do you feel from your spouse? Are you speaking your spouse's love language? If you don't know the love language of your spouse, request that both of you take the free quiz at *www.5lovelanguages.com* and discuss the results.

7. In the first three years, you will not know the primary love language of your child. So you speak all five love languages.

At around three years of age, you can observe their behavior and likely discover their primary love language. Give heavy doses of their primary language and sprinkle in the other four and your child will grow up feeling loved. Few things are more important for the emotional health of your child.

I Wish I'd Known . . .

That Children Are **GREATLY INFLUENCED** *by Our Model*

The most sobering question I have ever asked myself is: *What if my children turn out to be just like me?* I did not ask that question before they were born, nor when they were infants and toddlers. I asked that question a few years later when I began to see in them some of the traits that I saw in myself; some positive and some not so positive. The soberness of that question helped me make many decisions.

The hard reality is that there is every possibility that your children may turn out to be much like you. We know that the greatest single influence on children is the model of their parents. Certainly you want to verbally teach your children to be kind, courteous, patient, forgiving, humble, generous, and honest. You want to expose them to books that teach such virtues. However, your model is far more important than your words. Children are influenced far more by what you do than by what you say.

The closer your behavior matches what you teach them verbally, the greater respect your children will have for you. The larger the gap between what you teach and what you practice, the less respect they will have for you.

> The hard reality is that there is every possibility that your children may turn out to be much like you.

That does not mean that you must be perfect, but it does mean that you must apologize for your failures and ask forgiveness. (More about this in chapter 8.)

The old saying, "Do as I say, not as I do," may make you feel "in charge," but it will not develop character in your child. What you do speaks so loudly that they cannot hear what you say. However, when your actions reflect the things you teach, then your words enhance the child's understanding of what you are saying.

So I invite you to be brave and ask yourself the following questions. What if my child grows up to:

Handle anger the way I handle anger?

Treat their spouse the way I treat my spouse?

Drive a car the way I drive a car?

Have the same work ethic that I have?

Talk to other people the way I talk to others?

Handle conflicts the way I handle conflicts?

Respond to alcohol and drugs the way I do?

Have the same quality of relationship with God that I have?

Handle their money the way I handle my money?

Treat their in-laws the way I treat mine?

Treat their children the way I am treating them?

You may want to add a few questions of your own.

Okay, so I have started this chapter on a really somber note, but I have done so because I hope you will ask these kinds of questions much earlier than I did. In fact, now is the best time to ask and answer these questions. If you need to make changes in your own attitudes and lifestyle choices, why not begin to make those changes before the baby is born, or before they get old enough for you to see your negative traits being reflected in their behavior.

Remembering your childhood

Maybe an easier place to start is to examine your own childhood experience. Most of us have some happy childhood memories and some not so happy. It is always easier to start with positive memories. One of my positive memories is working with my father in our vegetable garden. He taught me how to plant corn, okra, squash, tomatoes, potatoes, turnips, and peppers. I can still visualize all of those plants growing in our garden. Looking back, I realize that I learned much of my work ethic from my father.

Shannon shared with me one of her positive childhood memories. "My mother played the organ at our church and regularly practiced at home. We sang at church. We sang at home. I fondly remember listening to music and singing along to the radio in the car with my mother. I grew up in the '70s and '80s and still today love songs of that era. But as a child, I sang the songs of the '50s and '60s like they were current chart toppers, because that was largely what played on my mother's car radio. Still today, I find myself randomly singing classics like 'Chances Are' (Johnny Mathis) and 'Mr. Sandman' (The Chordettes).

"My mother regularly sang to me the wonderful, old, and familiar tune, 'You are my sunshine, my only sunshine.' I know each verse of that Jimmie Davis song, too, and sing the whole thing to my children today. At two years of age, Presley started singing along with me. Yes, I can see my mother singing to me as I sing to my children."

Many adults can recall such treasured childhood memories of how they bonded with their parents over things like music, sports, camping, reading, gardening, and cooking. We fell in love with many of the things our parents loved. We watched and gained a shared appreciation for much of what they valued. As Rodney Atkins sings, "I want to do everything you do, so I've been watching you."[1] This song, "Watching You," playfully illustrates how children want to be like their parents and, in fact, often do and say things that their parents do and say.

Of course, many adults also have painful childhood memories. Parents who argued with each other in front of the children or behind closed doors; the words still ring in the ears of their adult children. Other adults can still visualize the face of an alcoholic father who cursed them and said words that are still etched in their memory. There were some pleasant memories, but most of their childhood was filled with fear, hurt, anger, and insecurity. However, as adults, even the negative memories can be instructive. We now know what not to do if we want to be responsible parents.

I suggest that you make a list of all the positive traits you saw in your mother and father. Then ask: how many of these traits do I see in myself? Next, make a list of the negative traits that you observed in your parents. Then ask: how many of these traits do I see in myself? This exercise will help you see how strongly you have been influenced by the model of your parents.

We can be thankful for the positive influence of our parents, and we can begin to focus on changing those negative traits that we see in ourselves. We did not choose our parents, nor our childhood experiences, but we do not have to repeat the negative example of our parents. When we decide to change, we have all the help of God and friends. God is in the business of changing lives. Thousands of people have shared their experience of reaching out to God to give them power to change destructive habits and found His hand outstretched. Friends also will help us when we are willing to share our need. The Christian church, at its best, is a hospital where people find healing and health.

Five steps toward modeling

Shannon and I would like to offer the following five steps in becoming the model you would be happy for your children to emulate.

First, put your hand in the hand of God and *be honest about where you are on your journey.* Be honest with yourself, your spouse, and your closest friends. Honesty is the first step to change. This means that you must be willing to reflect upon your life. Ask the hard questions. What do I need to change in order to be the kind of model I would want my child to follow?

> The Christian church, at its best, is a hospital where people find healing and health.

Perhaps it would be easier to start with your positive traits. What are your strengths? What do you do well? You may want to look at the list of questions at the beginning of this chapter and ask, "In which of these am I doing well?" Or look at the seven character traits listed above: kindness, courtesy, patience, a forgiving spirit, humility, generosity, and honesty. Ask the same question:

"In which of these am I doing well?" Or, rate yourself on a scale of 0 to 10 as to how you are doing in each of these traits. I have never met a man or woman that did not have some positive traits. If you smiled at someone today, that is an expression of kindness. If you did not blow the horn when the light turned green, that is a sign of patience. Give yourself credit for the good things you see in yourself. Make a list of these positive traits and look at it daily as a reminder of what you want to continue doing.

Then, look at those same questions and character traits and make a list of those that you are not doing so well; things you would like to change. Identifying "points for growth" is the first step in being honest with yourself. If you are really brave, share your list with your spouse and let them know that you sincerely want to grow in these areas.

The second step is: *Monitor your progress.* Active monitoring requires that parents consciously observe themselves. Parents instinctively watch their children to ensure healthy, safe, and desired behaviors. Parents may not as frequently watch themselves, or if they do, they may disregard the influence or consequences of their behavior on their children. By monitoring themselves, parents can see more clearly if they are demonstrating what, by their definition, are positive or negative thoughts, feelings, words, and actions around their children.

For additional and perhaps more objective perspective, parents may consider not only monitoring themselves but asking other people whom they trust to share their perception of them. This outside feedback can help to confirm or challenge how parents perceive themselves. Almost always there will be a difference between how we perceive ourselves and how others perceive us. Don't get defensive when a friend shares that you appear to be angry most of the time, that you seldom smile. Breathe deeply and thank them for being honest with you. Tell them that you will give some thought to what they are saying. Just as we want our children to learn and grow in life, we too should want to learn and grow. Our openness to learning and growing can motivate our children to do the same.

Active monitoring also requires that parents watch their children. Specifically, parents should watch how their children react to various types of everyday events or interactions. What do their children say? What do they do? By observing and listening to their children's reactions, parents may be surprised to discover that their children do and say what their parents do and say.

This can be cute when a toddler says, "I love our new house," because he has heard his parent say this. It may be charming when a child says to his baby sister, "Good morning, Beautiful" because he has heard his parent say this. But children's words and behaviors may not be so charming when they are screaming or hitting their parents or other children because they have heard or seen their parents doing the same. It may also be frustrating to parents when their children won't comply with boundaries because the parents have not consistently and positively established and reinforced healthy boundaries. This is not to say that all children's thoughts, feelings, words, and behaviors are directly influenced only by their parents' model. Many other environmental factors and other people also influence children. However, as parents actively watch their children's behaviors, they will likely see the influence of their own behavior.

The third step is: *Make the most of "teachable moments."* By teachable moments, I mean those moments in the normal flow of life when a child is open to learning. Children learn best by concrete experience rather than abstract concepts. You can sit on the couch and teach a child to look both ways before they cross the street, but that lesson is more likely to be internalized as you stand on the street corner and say, "Let's look both ways, and make sure it is safe to cross the street." That is a "teachable moment."

You may teach your child that when we get angry we count to 25 before we say or do anything. That is a laudable anger management technique. But the child is not likely to do that unless they *hear* you counting to 25, and then explaining why you felt angry and how happy you are that you took time to cool down before talking. When they get angry, you may start counting with them and praise them as they count.

Teachable moments may come in both our failures and successes as parents. In our successes, we explain to the child why we did what we did. In our failures, we let the child know that what we did was not good, and that we are trying to learn how not to do that again. Teachable moments also come in those times when our children are obedient and disobedient. In moments of obedience, we praise them and thank them for being mature enough to follow the rule. In times of disobedience, we explain why what they did was wrong and then let them suffer the natural or logical consequences, which we discussed in the last chapter.

Shannon shared with me that when she is in the car with Avery, she will sometimes talk to him about safe driving. He is years away from driving, but this is a teachable moment. She talks to him about such things as patience at traffic lights, and not turning left when the sign says "No left turn." Of course, if you are going to talk with a child about safe driving, remember that your model is more important than your words.

Life is filled with "teachable moments." The parent who aspires to be a positive model will be looking for these moments when they are with their children.

The fourth suggestion is that you approach your parental role with an *attitude of love.* Life is a series of opportunities and challenges; both entail numerous benefits and burdens. When parents embrace this reality and view life through a lens of love, they will be better able to convey to their children the virtues of compassion, kindness, patience, and forgiveness, even when working through challenging issues.

Love is the opposite of selfishness. Selfishness views the world with the question: What am I getting out of this? Love views the world with the question: How can I enrich the lives of others? Self-

> Parents are wise to view themselves through a lens of love so they are not overly critical of themselves.

ishness ends up destroying relationships. Love is the essential ingredient for healthy relationships. Selfishness leads to manipulation: "I will do this for you if you will do this for me." Love leads to giving: "How may I help you?" Selfishness ultimately leads to isolation. Love leads to community. Love builds strong marriages. Two selfish people will never have a strong marriage. Your marriage becomes a model of love or selfishness, which will greatly influence your children.

Love is what most parents hope to convey to their children in good times and in tough times. We know children are exploring and learning. We know they are watching everything we do. We want them to grow up unafraid, feeling secure and loved, and thus able to more fully love themselves and others. Parents can help their children reach these goals by approaching parenting with a loving attitude.

Parents are wise also to view themselves through a lens of love so that they are not overly critical of themselves. To continually put yourself down because of past failures may render you incapable of loving in the present. You cannot change the past, but you can learn from it. You can acknowledge your failures, accept forgiveness from God and others, forgive yourself, and move into the future as a more loving person. When you live under the burden of past failures, you are not loving yourself; you are not enhancing your life, nor the life of your children. When you forgive yourself, you will more easily extend forgiveness to your children when they fail.

Both Shannon and I have counseled many parents who have put too much pressure on themselves in their efforts to be perfect parents. Such parents are relentless in their pursuit of perfection. They may not label their goal as "perfection," but they are quietly striving for just that. Some of these parents come to us asking that we help "fix" their children. Often we discover that it is not so much that the children are misbehaving or underachieving, as it is that the parents have unrealistic, inflexible expectations of their children. We commend them for their desire to see their children succeed, but try to help them set more realistic expectations. We encourage them to consider putting more energy into building a loving, positive relationship with their child. The child who feels loved will accomplish more of his/her potential than the child who feels badgered by parents.

The last suggestion for parents who would like to become a worthy model for their children is to consider writing a *vision and mission statement* for themselves as parents. We are far more likely to hit the target if we know what we want to accomplish. A vision statement gives the big-picture, overarching inspirational goal to which we aspire. A mission statement gives the more practical action steps and goals that are necessary to help accomplish the vision.

For example, here is a sample vision statement: "Our vision as parents is that our thoughts, feelings, words, and actions will consistently be loving, positive, encouraging, forgiving, and gracious. From our model, we hope that our children will learn over time that they also do not have to be perfect, but like us, can accept and grow from their shortcomings and failures."

A mission statement might read as follows: "Our mission as parents is that we daily see ourselves through the lens of love and teach our children to do the same. We commit to regularly monitoring our thoughts, feelings, words, and actions to ensure that they are consistently loving, positive, encouraging, forgiving, and gracious. We know we will fall short at times, but will openly acknowledge our shortcomings and actively take steps to improve. We will maintain reasonable, achievable expectations for ourselves as parents and for our children."

These sample vision and mission statements reflect awareness and acceptance of parents' great influence on children. Evidence of that influence is not difficult to observe; it is readily identifiable in the children's words and actions. Children are influenced by other sources as well. However, it is the parents, or primary caregivers, who have the earliest and most significant foundational influence in their lives. Because of the great influence that parents have on their children, it is important that parents intentionally and actively take steps to be the best parental model they can be for their children.

Again, I am not suggesting that parents must be perfect models. What I am suggesting is that we must seek to use both our strengths and weaknesses as vehicles for growth. We are all constantly changing, for better or for worse. The goal of responsible parents is to be improving in the areas where we are weak and making the most of our strengths. My hope is that the ideas in this chapter will help you become a worthy model for your children. I wish I had focused on these ideas before we became parents. I think I would have made significant changes much earlier.

Talking It Over

1. On a scale of 0–10 rate yourself on the following seven character traits.

   Kindness

   Courtesy

   Patience

   Forgiveness

   Humility

   Generosity

   Honesty

   Which of these would you most like to improve? What steps will you take? Focus on one of these traits each week for the next seven weeks.

2. Honestly answer the following questions with the words "happy" or "sad," indicating how you would feel.

What if my child grows up to:

Handle anger the way I handle anger?	
Treat their spouse the way I treat my spouse?	
Drive a car the way I drive a car?	
Have the same work ethic that I have?	
Talk to other people the way I talk to others?	
Handle conflicts the way I handle conflicts?	
Respond to alcohol and drugs the way I do?	
Have the same quality of relationship with God that I have?	
Handle their money the way I handle my money?	
Treat their in-laws the way I treat mine?	
Treat their children the way I am treating them?	

If you indicated "sad," then talk with your spouse and come up with a plan to initiate positive change.

3. What is the one thing you would most like to change before your child is born? Talk with your spouse, a friend, pastor, or counselor and get ideas on steps you can take to make that change a reality.

4. You don't have to be perfect to be a good model to your child. However, you must learn to apologize when you fail. More about this in chapter 8.

8

I Wish I'd Known . . .

That Sometimes PARENTS *Need to* APOLOGIZE

When I looked into the crib at our babies, I gave no thought to the concept of apologizing to them. I never intended to do anything to hurt them. I loved them from the moment they were born. As a father, I would protect them, teach them, pray for them, and do everything in my power to see that they had a good life. Reflecting back on those days, I realize that I was naive to think that I would never need to apologize—that I would be a perfect father.

Why do we sometimes hurt the people we love the most? Because we are human. All of us are broken. We were born of parents who were broken. There are no perfect humans, though one man did raise his hand when the speaker asked, "Does anyone know of a perfect husband?" He shot his hand right up and said, "My wife's first husband." My observation is, if there are perfect husbands, they are deceased, and most of them became perfect after they died. The reality is we are all human, and from time to time we say and do things that hurt our spouses and children and fracture our relationships.

> Why do we sometimes hurt the people we love the most? Because we are human.

The good news is that our failures need not destroy our relationships if we are willing to apologize and they are willing to forgive. Apologizing and forgiving are essential to maintaining good relationships. Children need to learn these skills because they too will not be perfect.

At the age of five our granddaughter, who was visiting us, asked her grandmother, "May I have some stickers?" She knew that Karolyn had a "sticker drawer." Karolyn said to Davy Grace, "Certainly. You may have three stickers. You can choose any three that you like." Karolyn went about her business, and approximately thirty minutes later I walked in the house and saw stickers all over the house. They were on chairs, doors, and drawers. One was on the oven door, another on the refrigerator. I said to Karolyn, "Why all the stickers?" She looked around and realized what had happened. She said to Davy Grace, "You disobeyed Grandmother. I told you that you could have three stickers. You have taken many and placed them all around the house." Davy Grace began to cry and said, "I need somebody to forgive me." Of course, Karolyn wrapped her arms around her and said, "Grandmother forgives you. I love you so much."

Davy Grace spoke for the human race when she said, "I need somebody to forgive me." This is one of the fundamental realities that must be embraced if we are to have healthy relationships. Apologizing is the first step in finding forgiveness, and forgiveness heals broken relationships.

Yet some of us were taught not to apologize. I remember the young man who said to me, "My father said, 'Real men don't apologize.'" I said to him, "Your father was probably a good man, but he got some bad information. The reality is, real men must apologize if they are to have good marriages and be good parents. The same is true of real women."

Part of the problem is that we have different ideas as to what it means to apologize. I remember the wife sitting in my office with her husband. She said, "I would forgive him if he would apologize." To which he responded, "I did apologize." She said, "You did not apologize." He said, "I told you I was sorry." She retorted, "That is not an apology." Obviously, she was looking for something more than, "I'm sorry."

Most of us learned to apologize or not to apologize from our parents. My guess is that the man in the paragraph above, when he was a child, pushed his sister down the stairs and his mother said, "Johnny, don't push your sister down the stairs. Go tell her you're sorry." So little Johnny said, "I'm sorry." He's now twenty-eight, and realizing that he has offended his wife, he says, "I'm sorry." In his mind, he has apologized. However, her mother taught her a different way of apologizing. She said, "When you realize that you've hurt someone, always say, 'I was wrong. I should not have done that. I hope that you will forgive me.'" These are the words she is waiting for her husband to say. However, those words have never crossed his mind.

Languages of apology

A few years ago, Dr. Jennifer Thomas and I wrote a book entitled *When Sorry Isn't Enough.*[1] In our research, we asked thousands of people two questions:

1. When you apologize, what do you typically say or do?

2. When someone apologizes to you, what do you want to hear them say or do? Their answers fell into five categories, which we call the five languages of apology. Briefly, let me describe each of these, because I believe all five need to be taught to your children.

1) *Expressing Regret—"I'm sorry."* However, those two words should never be spoken alone. Tell the person what you are sorry for. "I'm sorry that I lost my temper and yelled at you. I'm sorry that I took your toy without asking. I'm sorry that I knocked your blocks down." Another important factor—never put the word "but" after you say "I'm Sorry." "I'm sorry that I lost my temper with you, but if you had not . . . then I would not have lost my temper." Now you are blaming them for your poor behavior.

2) *Accepting Responsibility—"I was wrong and should not have done that"* or "no excuse for that, I accept full responsibility." Helping a child accept responsibility for his/her behavior is fundamental to learning how to apologize. My son was six or seven years old when he accidentally knocked a glass off the table. It fell to the floor and broke. I looked at him and he said, "It did it by itself!" I said, "Let's say that a different way. 'I accidentally knocked the glass off the table.'" With tears in his eyes, he said, "I accidentally knocked the glass off the table."

What he did was not wrong. It was an accident. I was just trying to help him accept responsibility for his behavior.

3) *Offering to Make Restitution*—*"What can I do to make things right?"* or "What can I do to make it easier for you to forgive me?" For some people, if you do not offer to make things right, then you have not apologized. For a child, this may mean offering to rebuild the wall of blocks they intentionally kicked over.

4) *Expressing the Desire to Change*—*"I don't like what I did and I don't want to do it again.* I'm going to put a sign on my desk that says, 'Don't go into Erick's room without knocking and asking, "May I come in?"' I think that will help me remember." Expressing the desire to change communicates deeply to some people that you are sincere in your apology.

5) *Requesting Forgiveness*—*"Will you please forgive me?"* Or "I hope you will forgive me." For some people this communicates that you value the relationship. You realize that you have hurt them, that your behavior has put a barrier between the two of you. You sincerely hope that they will forgive you so that you can continue to be friends.

What Dr. Thomas and I discovered is that most adults did not learn to speak all five of these apology languages when they were children. Most learned only one or two. Thus, as an adult they apologize using the language they were taught. They fail to realize that it may not be connecting with the person to whom they are apologizing. This is why husbands and wives often miss each other in their efforts to apologize, and thus find it hard to forgive.

I suggest that you and your spouse discuss your perspectives on what constitutes a sincere apology. Learning how to give an apology in a manner that is meaningful to your spouse may help you find it easier to forgive each other. Of course, you may discover that one of you almost never apologizes for anything. Perhaps your dad also said, "Real men don't apologize." If so, may I encourage you to love your father—but reject this advice. If you don't learn to apologize, you will handicap your children socially and have a fractured relationship with your spouse.

Remember, as we discussed in chapter 7, your model is the best way to teach your children to apologize. So yes, I am suggesting that you learn to apologize to your children. Some parents feel that if they apologize, their children will lose respect for them. The opposite is true—they gain respect for you. They already know that what you did or said was wrong.

What should you apologize for?

So what are the kinds of actions that call for a parent to apologize to a child? Let's begin with the unkind things you say or do directly to your children. Parents may take out their own frustrations on the child with harsh, loud words, which deliver critical, condemning messages. If parents do not apologize, these messages often linger in the child's mind for years. Failing to listen or pay attention when a child is talking or otherwise trying to engage you, the parent, also calls for an apology. Some parents may at times wrongly punish their child because they failed to get all the facts about the situation. Others punish the child excessively when another form of discipline would have sufficed.

Another category of adult behavior that may call for an apology to children is things we do and say that indirectly negatively affect our children. Parents who loudly and harshly argue with each other in front of their children, without concern for their children's thoughts and emotions, definitely need to apologize to their children (and their spouse). Also included in this category are those times when parents mistreat another person and the children hear or see it. (Such as the way you talk to the telemarketer who calls trying to sell you vinyl siding for your brick house.) Another example of indirectly offending your child is when parents fail in their basic responsibilities such as work, housekeeping, providing food, and safety for their children. Addiction of any kind—substance abuse, gambling, etc.—often leads parents to neglect their parental role and calls for an apology.

By sharing these examples, my goal is not to induce guilt or shame. Instead, I want to encourage parents to be aware of and capitalize on their opportunities to apologize to their children whenever appropriate. When parents value apology and commit to apologizing as needed, they are teaching their children one of the fundamental skills needed for healthy relationships.

How apologizing helps

So, what are the benefits of learning to apologize to your children? Let me suggest three key positive results.

Apologies build and demonstrate character

Parents are typically interested in building their children's character; that is, their ability to face life's challenges with mental and moral strength. Character is something children begin to develop while young and then continue throughout adulthood. Parents, too, must continually maintain and build character as they encounter their own challenges, including times when they make parenting mistakes that directly or indirectly negatively affect their children.

Learning from our mistakes builds character in and of itself. To learn from mistakes means that parents reflect on and accept responsibility for their mistakes. They then seek to avoid similar mistakes in the future. This process of reflection, acceptance of fault, and commitment to improvement builds parents' character.

By learning from their mistakes, parents model for their children the importance of dealing effectively with our failures. For example, the parent who recognizes and controls his or her temper by taking a time-out models for the child self-control. This is a character-building practice. Or, if a parent reacts angrily but, after personal reflection, takes time to accept responsibility and apologize, they are demonstrating character and modeling it for the child.

> Learning from our mistakes builds character.

Shannon shared with me the story of a father who felt concerned about his long-term angry outbursts. Deeply convicted of his poor behavior, he apologized to his entire family. His twelve-year-old son was somewhat shocked because he had never had anyone ask his forgiveness before. That was a life-altering and family-altering point in their family.

Apologies build and restore relationships

In the family, we cannot treat each other harshly and expect to have wholesome family relationships. Children and spouses often suffer in silence after an altercation. Healing does not come with the passing of time. Healing comes when we admit our failures, apologize, and ask forgiveness. Shannon tells her own experience in the following story.

"Not long after Presley turned two years old, she and I were in the kitchen having a snack when she accidentally knocked over my cup of chocolate milk. To my shame, I impulsively snapped at her. I remember thinking, as the words were coming out of my mouth, 'I should not be overreacting.' I knew that I was stressed about other matters and that I was taking my stress out on Presley. She, of course, didn't know or care about my stress. She merely knew she had displeased me, and that I in turn, hurt her feelings. With tears in her eyes, she went to Stephen for consoling.

"I waited a few minutes to allow Presley time to settle. I then held her and told her, 'Presley, I am so sorry. I shouldn't have yelled at you.' She hugged me back, and with sweet, muddled language, she repeated my words: 'Shouldn't yell at me?' She seemed to say this as if asking me the question, 'You shouldn't yell at me, right?' She repeated these words to me a few more times over the course of the day. She was engaging in relationship restoration. Older children ask a similar question: 'Are you still mad at me?' These and similar words illustrate how children check in with their parents after conflict to ensure their relationship is still intact and that they are again accepted by their parents."

When parents fail to demonstrate kindness and fairness, children may feel emotionally distanced, disliked, or even hated by their parents. Children can experience emotional reconnection, as well as resolution of negative feelings, when parents genuinely apologize and then consistently work to avoid the same types of hurtful mistakes in the future.

Of course, we know that forgiveness is not always automatic for adults or children. Because of this, parents should not unfairly expect their children to immediately forgive their worst mistakes. However, we also know that the act of thoughtful, sincere apology combined with consistently positive interactions across time can help restore even the most damaged relationships.

Apologies teach children how to deal with their own failures

Children will not be perfect. They will sometimes break the rules, speak harshly to parents or siblings, push or kick another child, etc. I know it is hard to imagine this when you hold your infant in your arms, but it will happen. Children are not by nature apologizers. Rather, they are blamers. Have you noticed this same trait in yourself? It is much easier to blame your spouse than accept responsibility for your own failure.

You alone know if you process your own failures in a healthy manner. Many adults are not good apologizers. They can say harsh things to their spouse or others, walk away, in their minds blame the other person for their poor behavior, and never return to apologize. A series of such unresolved offenses often leads to the breakup of the relationship.

Five steps toward learning to apologize

If you are going to teach your child to apologize, you must first learn how to apologize yourself. The best time for you to learn this is before your child is born or while they are very young. So let me give you the five steps in learning to apologize and encourage you to see where you are in these important steps. Incidentally, these are the same five steps you will need to teach your children.

1. *Accept responsibility for your own actions.*

"I left the garage door open. I forgot to take out the trash. I broke the dish. I tracked in mud. I spoke harshly to you. I lost my temper. I was unkind. I forgot to pick up the milk." Not all of these are moral failures. Some are simply human ineptness. The point is simply taking responsibility for your behavior.

2. *Your actions affect others.*

No man is an island. What I do, good or not so good, affects those around me. If I come home two hours late when we had agreed to attend the symphony, I have disappointed my spouse. When I clean the garage, my spouse will likely be elated. If in anger I speed down the highway at ninety miles per hour, my spouse will experience fear. Everything we do, good or bad, impacts other people.

3. *There are always rules in life.*

We often think of making rules for our children's safety (which we discussed earlier), but adults also have rules we must follow for our own well-being. Without rules a society descends into chaos. When I obey the rules, life is much easier. When I disobey rules, there will be negative consequences. The greatest of all rules is: "Do unto others as you would have them do unto you," sometimes called the Golden Rule.

4. *Apologies will restore friendships.*

We have all observed broken relationships: in the home, at work, with extended family, or with neighbors. Most of these are the results of failure to apologize and forgive. When we apologize, we open the door to the possibility of forgiveness. When they forgive, the relationship is restored.

5. *We must learn to speak our apologies in a way that is meaningful to the person we offended.*

This is where the five apology languages we discussed earlier in this chapter are helpful. Most adults have not learned to speak all five of these languages.

However, it is never too late to learn. Read the following

list and assess how fluent you are in speaking each of these.

"I'm sorry that I . . ."

"I was wrong."

"What can I do to make it right?"

"I'll try not to do that again."

"I hope you will forgive me."

Children need to learn all five languages of apology, but they are not likely to do so, unless parents speak them. If these seem unnatural to you, then I suggest that you stand in front of a mirror and say them aloud, until they begin to feel a bit more comfortable. The more often you repeat them, the more likely you are to speak them when you really do need to apologize to your spouse or a coworker.

However, apology alone does not restore relationships. Apology is the first step, but apology must be met with forgiveness if the emotional barrier is to be removed. When I accept your apology, I am choosing to forgive you. Forgiveness may be easy or difficult based on many factors such as the nature and frequency of the offense and the perceived sincerity of the apology. Forgiveness is also influenced by how well the person learned to apologize and forgive when they were children. When parents apologize and forgive each other, not only do they enhance their own relationship, but they also model the process for their children.

I wish I had learned to apologize much earlier. Many of the marital struggles Karolyn and I had in the early years could have been avoided if I had been willing to accept responsibility for my words and actions; admitted my wrong; offered to make it up to her; worked at not repeating the same destructive actions; and requested forgiveness. I hope that this chapter will help you grow in the willingness and ability to apologize and to forgive. Again I ask, "What if my children turn out to be just like me?"

Talking It Over

1. When did you last apologize to anyone? How did you express your apology? How did the person respond? Are you pleased with the outcome? After reading this chapter, how might you have reframed your apology?

2. What did your parents teach you about apologizing?

3. Do you ever remember your parents apologizing to you? If not, what are some things for which you wish they had apologized?

4. Look at the following apology languages and check the one or two that you consider to be a sincere apology.

	Expressing regret— "I'm sorry that I . . ."
	Accepting responsibility— "I was wrong. I should not have done that."
	Offering to make restitution— "What can I do to make things right?"
	Expressing the desire to change— "I don't like what I did and I don't want to do it again."
	Requesting forgiveness— "Will you please forgive me?"

5. Discuss with your spouse what they consider to be a sincere apology. Share with your spouse what you consider to be a

sincere apology. Can you see how you may have missed each other emotionally by speaking the wrong apology language?

6. When is the last time you apologized to your spouse? How did he/she respond?

7. When is the last time your spouse apologized to you? How did you respond?

8. How successful have you been in forgiving your spouse after they apologize? What might they do that would make it easier for you to forgive them? Share this information with your spouse.

9. Learning to apologize effectively to your spouse and your child is essential if you are to have healthy family relationships. This is one of the basic social skills that your child needs to learn. (More about social skills in chapter 9.)

9

I Wish I'd Known . . .

That SOCIAL SKILLS
Are as Important as
ACADEMIC SKILLS

M any parents believe that academic success is their child's ticket to the "good life." What many parents do not realize is that As on the report card do not necessarily translate to success in life. Without healthy social skills, an "A" student may live a "C" or "D" lifestyle. Many of the people who are fired from their jobs did not lose their jobs because of intellectual deficiencies but because they could not get along with people. Most couples who divorce are intelligent people, but they never learned how to resolve conflicts without arguing; how to keep emotional love alive after the "in-love" euphoria faded; how to make requests rather than demands; and numerous other challenges that require social skills.

I am not downplaying the importance of academic skills. We

will discuss this more fully in chapter 10. What I am saying is that academic skills are not enough to succeed in life. Most vocations involve working with other people. "People skills" may well make the difference between success and failure. In this chapter I want to identify some of the social skills that are necessary for success, and how you as a parent can help your child develop these skills.

When our children were young, I knew that I wanted them to be loving, kind, responsible, hardworking, and well-mannered. I wanted them to be able to process their own emotions in a healthy manner and to respect the emotions of others. I wanted them to be friendly and able to engage others in conversation. I wanted them to discover that the greatest satisfaction in life is found in serving others. However, I must be honest, I gave little thought as to how I would help them develop these traits. I relied mostly on wishful thinking.

> "People skills" may well make the difference between success and failure.

What I want to share with you are some of the things I learned along the way, in my studies, in my counseling office, and in rearing my own children. I will also draw from Shannon's experiences and training.

How a child learns empathy

Let me begin with *empathy*—the ability to enter into the feelings of others and identify with their pain or joy. This is one of the basic skills necessary for a counselor. There are no successful counselors who do not have empathy. However, there are many adults who do not have this skill. They never learned how to acknowledge and name their own emotions. Therefore, they have difficulty understanding the emotions of others. They will not be very supportive of a coworker who experiences disappointment, sadness, or trauma. Their basic approach is to keep their distance from those who are experiencing pain. They may be good, honest people, but they do not have this social skill.

How, then, do you teach your child to empathize with others? It begins with your seeking to identify with *their* emotions. When an infant cries, you move to the child, seeking to discover why they are crying. They cannot talk, so in the early days it is a guessing game. Cries may mean they are hungry, need a diaper change, in pain, tired, bored, or simply in need of human touch. As time moves on, you will learn how to distinguish between various types of cries. Through patient, persistent, and empathetic response to their baby's cries, the parent can both successfully meet their baby's basic needs and successfully establish the foundation of social connectedness with their children. This model is the first step in teaching your child to have empathy for others.

As children move into the toddler and talking stage, parents have more clues as what their children are feeling. One of the parent's roles is to attach words to the child's emotions. When a toddler falls down and begins to cry, as the parent hugs the child they may say, "Did my baby get hurt? Show Mommy where it hurts." As the months and years go by, parents continue to help children develop an emotional vocabulary. The child must learn to identify his/her own emotions before they can learn to have empathy for the emotions of others.

Eventually children come to the stage that they begin to identify with the emotions of parents. When a mother says, "I feel sad when you disobey me," and, the child responds, "I'm sorry, Mommy," the child is now empathizing with the mother. It is a slow process, but talking about emotions, both yours and theirs, is the road to developing the important social skill of empathy.

Showing and teaching kindness

A second social skill is *kindness*—words and deeds that enhance the lives of others. The child who learns to express kindness will not only enrich others but will also find great satisfaction. Albert Schweitzer, who as a physician invested his life in what was then French Equatorial Africa, was awarded the Nobel Peace Prize in 1952. In his acceptance speech he said, "One thing I know: the only ones among you who will be really happy are those who will have sought and found how to serve."[1]

When you teach your child to be kind, you are giving him or her one of the most important social skills. It all begins when you are kind to your child. When you speak kind words in a friendly tone of voice, you are teaching by your model. When you do things that you believe will enhance your child's life, you are demonstrating kindness. All children will respond positively to kindness.

Once you have established this pattern, then you can say to the child, "Do you remember how good you felt when I told you how proud I was of you? Let's think of something kind we can say to your grandmother." Your child will likely get excited and start coming up with ideas of what he wants to say. Or you might say, "Do you remember how happy Mom was when you and I cleaned the garage? Let's think of something else we can do for her that will make her happy." Acts of kindness and words of kindness will serve your child well in the adult world.

The art of saying "Thank you"

A third social skill is *gratitude*—the art of saying "Thank you." When children learn to say "Thank you," they are developing a social skill that will enhance their relationships greatly as they grow up. A school cafeteria worker once said to me, "I serve about 300 children at lunch every day. Only ten of them ever say 'thank you' as I serve them. It is always the same ten. They make my day." How would you like for your child to be one of the ten?

It all begins with your model. When you thank your spouse for a meal they prepared, your child will likely follow your example. When you say to your children, "Let's all thank Dad or Mom for working today so that we can have a house in which to live," you are teaching them that the things we enjoy didn't just happen. Someone worked to make them happen. Grateful children typically grow up with grateful parents.

You might also play the "thanksgiving game" with young children who are old enough to talk. Everyone gets in one room and we take turns expressing thanks for various items we see in the room. For example, "I am thankful for this chair." Another says, "I am thankful for the rug." See how many things you can give thanks for in ten minutes. Little children really get into this game, and every time they say "I am thankful for . . . ," they are developing the skill of gratitude.

When is the last time you said "Thank you" to anyone? If you can't remember, then perhaps you need to set a goal of saying it to at least three people each day. If you do not have this social skill, you are not likely to teach it to your child.

> Grateful children grow up with grateful parents.

A fourth social skill is *focused attention*—giving someone your undivided attention. My wife, Karolyn, keeps this on the front burner of my mind when she says, "Wherever you are, be all there." In today's world, multitasking is lauded as a way to save time. However, multitasking does not build relationships. When you are watching TV or are on social media, has your spouse ever said, "Would you please listen to me?" Your response may have been, "I am listening to you." The truth is that it is possible to watch TV and listen to your spouse, but that is not focused attention. What your spouse is asking for is your undivided attention.

When you give someone your undivided attention, you are communicating that you think they are important, that you value their thoughts, ideas, and feelings. When you give them eye contact while they are talking, ask questions to make sure you understand, express affirmation, and then share your perspective, you are demonstrating one of the most important skills in developing relationships: focused attention.

The ability to focus one's attention has many other benefits. Children who can "pay attention" in school will do better academically. (More about this in chapter 10.) Those children who play sports will excel if they can focus attention on the task at hand. In almost every area of life, children who can concentrate on one task at a time will be more successful than those children who get easily distracted. Of course, some children suffer from Attention Deficit Disorder and will need professional help.

So where do parents begin to teach this social skill? I believe it begins when they are infants, by giving them your undivided attention. I don't mean twenty-four hours per day but extended periods of talking to the child, singing to the child, holding or cuddling the child: these are the kind of activities that lay the foundation for focused attention.

As the child gets older, reading to your child helps develop their attention span. Some parents make the mistake of putting screens in front of their children at a very early age. But screens diminish the ability to concentrate, because they are constantly changing. In fact, the American Academy of Pediatrics recommends that parents avoid television viewing and screen time for children under the age of two.[2]

As children get older, screen time must continue to be limited and monitored. Unlimited screen time will not help a child learn the social skill of focused attention. What it does teach is that life should be constantly interesting, instant, and rewarding. Real life and real people do not always have these qualities. Children who get addicted to screens will not develop the social skill of focused attention.

On the other hand, the more you play age-appropriate games with your child that require eye contact, conversation, and thought, the more your child will learn how to feel comfortable with people. Game times are the laboratory for developing your child's social skills.

> I might also warn parents about their own tendency to get distracted.

Conversations with your child are also key to developing the skill of focused attention. When you talk with your child, be sure to make eye contact and teach them to do the same. I might also warn parents about their own tendency to get distracted. When you are talking with your child and your cellphone rings, and you answer it, you are saying to your child, "This person is more important than you." As parents we too must practice focused attention.

A fifth social skill is *common courtesies*—things we do and don't do when relating to people. Recently I was met at the airport by a young man who was taking me to my hotel. I was to speak at his business that evening. As we rode, I noticed that he responded to my questions with "Yes, sir" or "No, sir." I assumed that he must have recently served in the military, but I was wrong.

That evening when I heard him speaking to a woman at the meeting, his response was either, "Yes, ma'am" or "No, ma'am." It was obvious to me that he had been raised in a home where he had been taught this common courtesy: address a man as "sir" and a woman as "ma'am."

Each culture and subculture has its own list of common courtesies. Usually, these are taught and learned in the home. Here are a few of the common courtesies I learned growing up in a middle-class working family in the Southeast United States.

When someone gives you a compliment or a gift, always say, "Thank you."

Don't talk with food in your mouth.

Ask permission before playing with your sister's toys.

Don't take the biggest piece of chicken.

When it comes to food, taste it before you reject it. Then say, "I don't care for that. Thank you."

Never enter someone's room without knocking. Then say, "May I come in, please?"

Do your chores before you play ball.

When you see your mother or father doing something, always ask, "May I help you?"

Wait your turn to ride the scooter.

When Aunt Zelda arrives, meet her at the door with a hug.

If you want Johnny to come out to play, knock on the front

door and ask his mother, "May Johnny come out and play with me?" If she says, "Not now," say, "Thank you." And leave.

Say "Yes, ma'am" or "No, ma'am" to your mother and "Yes, sir" and "No, sir" to your father.

Don't scream at your parents or your sister.

When someone else is talking, don't interrupt.

When you enter the house, take off your cap.

Look a person in the eye when you speak to him or her.

When you want salt at the dinner table, say, "Please pass the salt."

When you leave the dinner table, say, "May I please be excused?"[3]

All of these "common courtesies" are designed to show respect for family members and neighbors. They are not universal norms, but they are common enough that you may have recognized a few that you were taught as a child. I am not suggesting that you adopt this list, but I am encouraging you to have a list of common courtesies that you plan to teach your child.

Public school teachers commonly tell me that the greatest problem they have in the classroom is lack of respect. Many students do not respect the teacher's authority, nor do they respect their fellow students. This often leads to disruption in the classroom.

Teaching your child common courtesies is the primary way to teach them respect for authority, property, and the rights of others. Children need to learn that there are certain things that we do and don't do because we respect one another. If the child learns to respect parents and siblings, he/she is more likely to respect teachers and other adults. The teenage son who screams at his parents will likely scream at his wife someday.

I would encourage you and your spouse to make a list of the common courtesies you were taught as a child. Examine the list and decide which of these you would like to teach your child. If you grew up in a home where little attention was given to being courteous, then talk with other couples and find out what courtesies they are teaching their children. Making a list is one way of keeping this social skill on the front burner of your mind.

Once you have the list, you might begin to observe how the two of you are expressing common courtesy to each other. Are you listening to each other with empathy, seeking to understand their perspective? Do you make requests rather than demands? When you have a conflict, do you focus on finding a solution rather than winning an argument? Before you request a change, do you first tell your spouse three things you like about them? Once you have heard their apology and chosen to forgive, do you let the incident be history? Just a few things to think about. Remember, your model of courtesy will be extremely important to your children.

> Children need to learn that there are certain things we do and don't do because we respect one another.

A sixth social skill is *anger management*—controlling my anger instead of letting it control me. All children experience the emotion of anger, as do all adults. The problem is not anger but how we handle anger. Children who don't learn how to respond to anger in a healthy manner will have relationship problems.

Unfortunately, many parents did not learn this social skill as a child and are still struggling with their own anger management.

Let's start at the beginning. There are two kinds of anger: definitive and distorted. Definitive anger is our emotional response when we are treated unfairly. Distorted anger is our response when we don't get what we want. Much of a child's anger is distorted anger. By two years of age, children may have temper tantrums, usually because they did not get the candy bar or toy that they wanted. It often happens in the store and can be terribly embarrassing to parents.

In order to get the child to calm down, parents often yield to the child's desire, grab the candy or toy, give it to the child, and say, "Okay, now stop screaming." In so doing, they are teaching the child that a temper tantrum will get them what they want. If this pattern continues, look for a rebellious teen and an out-of-control adult.

So how should a parent respond to this situation? I suggest that you never cave in to a temper tantrum. If it happens in a store, you simply take the child to the car and sit with them until they calm down. Tell them that is not the way to get a candy bar, that they will never get a candy bar by crying and screaming. Then take them back into the store and finish your shopping. If the tantrum happens at home, you tell them that if they want to scream, they can do it in their room, but not in your presence. Bottom line: don't let their angry, out-of-control behavior get them what they want. The child will soon learn to make requests, not demands, and when a parent says no, they will come to respect authority. Obviously, this kind of parental response should be done with calmness and love for the child.

Once you have passed the "temper tantrum test" and the

child gets old enough to talk, you can begin teaching the child a positive way to handle anger. We want to talk about our anger rather than screaming or pushing the person at whom we are angry. So, a mother might say, "When you are angry at me, I want you to come to me and say, 'Mommy, I'm angry, can we talk?' If I am washing dishes, I will say, 'Yes, as soon as I finish with the dishes.' If I am not busy, I will say, 'Yes, let's sit down and talk.' Now, what are you angry about?" You can then listen to the child with empathy and try to find a resolution.

If the child finds that you will listen to their complaints, they will learn to talk instead of yell. As the parent, your responsibility is to help them understand the difference between definitive anger and distorted anger. If you have indeed treated the child unfairly, then you need to apologize as we discussed in chapter 8. If, on the other hand, the child is angry because you are not allowing them to do something or will not give them something, you can explain your reasons and make the decision that you believe is best for the child. Remember, you are the parent and you know better than the child what is best for him/her. Of course, if they don't get their way, the child may still cry and walk off in a huff, but at least they know why you are doing what you are doing.

We cannot keep our children from crying when disappointed. In fact, such crying can be helpful. As adults we sometimes cry when we don't get what we want. But hopefully, as adults, we are not going to scream and throw bottles because we did not get our way. As we discussed in chapter 7, our model is extremely important. Therefore, if you don't handle your anger in a responsible manner, then it is time for you to take a course on anger management or read a book on the topic. For further help on understanding and processing anger, see my book *Anger: Taming a Powerful Emotion*.[4]

The good news is that we are never too old to learn. In fact, we must learn positive anger-management skills if we expect to teach our children how to manage their anger.

Two additional social skills that are extremely important for children are how to apologize and how to give and receive love. We have already looked at those extensively so we will not dwell on these here—but be aware of their great importance.

I wish I had known these social skills before we became parents. I must confess that I was well into the journey of parenting before I learned anger management. I was a bit better at some of the others, but always there was room for growth. I am convinced that the more you develop these skills in your own life, the more effective you will be in teaching them to your children.

Talking It Over

1. What are some of the emotions you have felt today? What stimulated these emotions? Getting in touch with your own emotions is the first step in teaching your child to have empathy for others.

2. Ask your spouse to share their answers to the above questions. This will get the two of you talking to each other on an emotional level.

3. What kind words have you spoken to someone today? What kind deeds did you perform for someone today? Ask your spouse to share their answer to these questions.

4. Set a goal of speaking a kind word or doing a kind deed to someone every day. You may want to start with your spouse.

5. Make a list of ten things for which you are thankful. Write these down and share them with your spouse. Add to the list

one thing for which you are grateful each day this week and share it with each other.

6. When your spouse is speaking, do you give them your full attention? Try sitting down one evening this week, with TV off, computer and phone shut down. Look at each other and share three things that happened in your life today and how you feel about them. Learning to give "focused attention" will prepare you for parenthood.

7. Make a list of the "common courtesies" you were taught as a child. Ask your spouse to do the same. Compare your lists and decide which of these you would like to teach your child. What else would you add to this list?

8. I hate to bring it up again, but how are you doing with anger management? If there is room for growth, perhaps you and your spouse could read and discuss a book on the topic. Mismanaged anger is detrimental to marriage and family relationships.

10

I Wish I'd Known . . .

That **PARKENTS** Are **RESPONSIBLE** for Their Child's **EDUCATION**

O h, I was big on education. I had finished my MA degree in education before our first child was born. I knew I wanted my children to have a good education. I assumed they would go to college. However, I did not give a lot of thought about my role in their education. I think I just assumed that was the role of schoolteachers. If you had asked me what our plans were for educating our children, I think I would have said, "I guess we will send them to public school. That's what my parents did, and it worked out pretty well."

I did not give serious thought to the reality that a whole lot of education takes place before they are old enough for first grade. Nor did I give thought to the fact that culture had changed greatly from the time I was in public school. (Not that I am anti-public school; more about that later.) I think Karolyn was more in touch with the children's educational needs than I was, and thankfully, she helped me get on board.

Your child's first teacher: you

Let me begin with some thoughts about educating children before they are old enough for kindergarten. Education has to do with the process of teaching and learning. Someone is teaching and someone is learning, and often the learning flows both ways. That was certainly true for me. As I taught my children, I was continually learning about them and from them. Much of the early education of children is done in the context of daily living. We may not be thinking "education," but we are "educating" by the way we respond to our children in the normal flow of life. This is illustrated in the story Shannon shares.

"Carson pushed Presley, causing her to fall on a concrete floor and bloody her knee. My first response was to console Presley and tend to her knee. This actually gave me time to collect my thoughts and decide how I wanted to deal with Carson's misbehavior. Carson watched as I tended to Presley's knee. His remorse was evident. Minutes later, I reminded him that he had caused Presley's accident. He said, 'I didn't know the floor would hurt her knee.' I hugged him and responded, 'You know now that the floor will hurt her knee. Do not push her again.' I encouraged Carson to apologize to Presley, which he did. From there we moved on from the incident—Presley with a bandaged knee and my validation of her physical and emotional pain; Carson with a lesson learned (I hope) and a demonstration of both my love for him and my willingness to hold him accountable; and me, with the immediate responsibility of preparing dinner even while wishing for a personal time-out."

In that brief life experience, Shannon taught Presley how to respond to a person who is hurting and taught Carson that concrete floors do hurt, that pushing people is wrong, and apologies are necessary when we do wrong. She also demonstrated that parents love children even when they misbehave. I doubt that Shannon was thinking, "I am educating my children," but that is exactly what she was doing. Parents are educators in every interaction they have with their children.

In addition to the many opportunities we have to teach in the normal flow of life, I would like to suggest that parents consciously create learning opportunities for their children. One of the earliest and easiest is to read to your child. This

> Parents are educators in every interaction they have with their children.

can begin as soon as he/she is able to sit on the couch beside you, or sit in your lap. Before they can understand the meaning of words, children can view the pictures, flip the pages, and get the idea that books are a part of life. When they begin to talk, you point to the picture of a cow and say, "cow." You are teaching your child vocabulary. They are associating the sound "cow" with the picture of a cow. They are not yet associating the sound "cow" with the printed word "cow." That will come later, but you are developing your child's vocabulary, which is a huge part of early education.

By the age of three many children can begin to learn to read. What I mean is that they can begin to associate printed words with their developing vocabulary. Yes, we used the flash card method, and it worked. This was Karolyn's idea, but I fully embraced the fun. I remember holding up the card with the word "toe" printed on it, and saying to our daughter "toe" while pointing to or touching her toe. She had the word "toe" in her vocabulary, but now she was making the connection between the printed word, the sound "toe," and her actual toe. Yes, she was learning to read. In today's technological world, you can Google "teach your child to read" and find all kinds of electronic products to help you with the process. As for me? I still like the flash cards.

What about preschool?

As I mentioned earlier, Karolyn and I made the decision that she would be a stay-at-home mom after our first child was born. So all of our children's education was done at home until they entered kindergarten. However, I am fully aware that in many families both mom and dad have full-time vocations, and other children are raised in single-parent homes, or preschool education is the custom in the community. In these settings, preschool childcare is necessary.

Shannon and Stephen were fortunate enough to have both sets of their parents nearby and willing to play a major role in childcare. This can be an excellent arrangement when parents are available and willing to do so. Who could be more concerned about the well-being of a child than the grandparents? When their children were between the ages of one and two, Shannon and Stephen enrolled their children in a half-day preschool program two or three mornings a week. This gave Shannon's mom, who was the primary caregiver, a break so she could run errands and tend to other personal interests.

In choosing a preschool childcare program, Shannon was fortunate to find a program that was more than simply childcare. It was truly educational, with staffers who were child-friendly, positive, and always looking out for the safety of the children. This leads me to urge parents to "do your homework" before you place your child in a preschool facility. Check the Internet to find out what is available in your area, but don't stop there. Talk to other parents who have children the age of your children, visit the sites and talk with childcare directors and staff, and observe classrooms. Yes, it will take time, but your efforts will be rewarded when you find a safe, friendly learning environment where your child can be cared for, nurtured, and educated.

Once you have made your selection and your child is enrolled in a preschool program, stay involved. Monitor and support those who are caring for your child. Typically, preschools welcome parents' involvement. Shannon also suggests that if your parents are playing a role in caring for your child, be sure to regularly check in with them to make sure they have what they need to care for your child. Don't take them for granted. Express appreciation often for the invaluable help they are to you and your children.

When thinking of the preschool education of your children, I would also like to note the key role that your local church can play in helping parents. Not all churches are the same. Some have excellent educational programs; others, not so much. Many churches offer daycare programs as well as Sunday learning experiences. When Karolyn and I moved to a new city where I was going to do graduate studies, we selected our church based on their preschool program. (I can put up with poor preaching, but I was not going to a church that did not have an excellent preschool program.) You may not presently be attending a church, but don't write off this valuable resource to help you in the education of your child.

Schooling options

Children steadily age out of the infancy, toddler, and preschool ages and reach the age at which they can be enrolled in kindergarten. I remember that day for both of our children. We had worked hard (I should say, Karolyn had worked hard) at finding the best kindergarten in town. We bought school supplies and book bags, took photos, and told the children what fun they were going to have. They were not disappointed, nor were we. (And, yes, there were a few tears when we realized that our "baby" was no longer a baby but was now officially "in school.") I don't know how many kindergartens still teach phonics, but we found that program to be excellent.

> I can put up with poor preaching, but I was not going to a church that did not have an excellent preschool program.

As your child enters kindergarten and then elementary school, the choices are many. When I was a child (many years ago), almost all children went to public schools. There were few—and in many cases, no—other options. That is not true today. Even in the public school sector, there are choices: traditional public schools, charter schools, and magnet schools. Then there are private schools: some with a religious orientation and some secular. Homeschooling is rising in popularity, and programs sometime include online classes and co-ops. Other options may appear in the next decade. The bottom line is that parents have an important decision to make in the education of their children. It will take time, effort, and much thought, but it will be one of the most important decisions you make for your child.

To gain an overview of the various types of schools and their objectives, you can search online. There are national organizations such as: US Department of Education, the National Education Association, the Council for American Private Education, National Home Education Research Institute, Association of Christian Schools International, and others. However, for more practical and local information, you may want to talk to other parents who have children in elementary schools. They can give you firsthand feedback based on their own experience.

Here is a brief overview of the various types of schools mentioned above.

Traditional public schools

Public schools differ greatly across the country. They range from excellent to chaotic, depending on location and leadership. One source of information is talking to teachers who teach in your local school system, and parents who have students enrolled in a school you might be considering. These schools follow the curriculum dictated by the local or state educational boards.

Charter schools

A charter school is an independently run public school granted greater flexibility in its operations, in return for greater accountability for performance. The "charter" establishing each school is a performance contract detailing the school's mission, program, students served, performance goals, and methods of assessment. Charter schools accept students by random, public lottery. Typically, charter schools have a high level of parental involvement.

Magnet schools

A magnet school is a public school with a focused theme and aligned curricula in Science, Technology, Engineering, and Mathematics (STEM). There are other themes as well, but these are foundational. Magnet schools are typically more "hands on—minds on" and use an approach to learning that is inquiry or performance/project based. They use state, district, or Common Core standards in all subject areas; however, they are taught within the overall theme of the school.

Private schools

According to the Council for American Private Education, there are 30,861 private schools in the United States, serving 5.3 million PK–12 students. Private schools account for 24 percent of the nation's schools and enroll 10 percent of all students. Most private school students (80 percent) attend religiously affiliated schools. Most private schools are small: 86 percent have fewer than three hundred students.

Parents choose a private school for many reasons: quality academics, a safe and orderly environment, moral and ethical values, caring teachers, and supportive communities. Parents who choose a Christian school are also motivated by the desire to see God and a Christian worldview integrated into academic studies. In choosing a private school, parents must consider the costs, which are considerably more than public schools.

Home schools

The homeschooling movement began growing in the 1970s as an alternative to public and private schools. Families choose to homeschool for a variety of reasons, including dissatisfaction with the educational options available, different religious beliefs or educational philosophies, and the belief that children are not progressing within the traditional school structure. According to the National Home Education Research Institute, there are now more than two million children being homeschooled in the US, with the percentage increasing by 7 percent to 15 percent each year. Homeschooling is legal in all fifty states.

I believe that most parents want to find the school that is best for their child. However, the road to making that discovery may be long. Sometimes the choices may be limited by various factors. A special-needs child may have few choices in a local community. Finances may also limit the choices available. Geography may diminish the number of options. The parent's worldview or philosophy of life may greatly impact their choice. The parent's own educational background and experience may influence their decision. What is the best school for *my* child? This is the question every parent must seek to answer.

> In my opinion, the elementary school years lay the foundation for the rest of the child's academic career.

How to decide?

Neither Shannon nor I want to try to answer that question for you. However, we would like to suggest some areas that you should investigate. The first is the curriculum the school is using. While public school systems tend to have a uniform curriculum in a given geographical area, they differ from state to state. Private schools, even when nationally accredited, retain more autonomy than individual public schools to determine their curricula.

Why is curriculum so important? Curriculum guides what children learn, including topics taught and how these topics are presented. This is a huge area of conflict in public education across the country. There is an effort on the part of some to rewrite history to make it more compatible with their own philosophical views. Another area of conflict is when and how to teach sex education. In some cases curriculum has become more socially oriented and the foundations of reading, writing, and arithmetic get lost in the efforts to be culturally relevant. These are important areas for parents to investigate. In my opinion, the elementary school years lay the foundation for the rest of the child's academic career. If they are deficient in reading, writing, and math, they will fight an uphill battle in middle school and high school and may never make it to college.

Parents should inquire about the philosophy behind the curriculum, how this philosophy will be implemented in the curriculum across various subjects, and what its targeted learning outcomes are. For those who are Christian parents, it is important to know the manner in which religion is treated in the curriculum. Does the curriculum ignore religious beliefs, or present a balanced view, or is it clearly anti-Christian? Various approaches are made by different curricula.

Many parents choose charter schools when this is an option because parents usually play a greater role in working with administration and staff in crafting the educational experience of their children. The same motivation often leads parents to enroll their children in magnet schools, especially when the child has a special educational focus.

Karolyn and I chose a Christian school for both of our children, kindergarten through the eighth grade. For high school we enrolled them in college preparatory private schools, which were not faith based. We have always been grateful for teachers and administrators who invested in their educational journey. We both felt strongly that we wanted our children taught from a Christian worldview. We shared with them other perspectives in our conversations, and why we had chosen the Christian faith. Both of them went on to college and graduate studies and as adults have a strong Christian faith with a deep desire to invest their lives in helping others.

Shannon and Stephen both grew up in public schools but have also chosen a private Christian school for their school-age children. She said, "This is a personal matter for us. We do not judge others for their choices of schools. However, we know what we want for our children and that includes our desire that they be taught religious faith and supported, not ridiculed or persecuted, for religious beliefs. We were not confident we could meet our goals in the public schools available to us."

I fully agree with Shannon and Stephen. Who you choose to help you educate your children is your choice and should be made in keeping with your values and philosophy.

Both Shannon and I highly recommend that once the school choice is made, that parents get involved with parent-teacher associations, volunteer at the school, attend school board meetings when allowed, and otherwise advocate for your child and his or her school. This proactive behavior can result in many positive educational and social outcomes for children, parents, schools, and communities.

Parents should regularly talk with their children about what they are learning at school and how it applies to life in the world around them. Discussion opportunities can emerge when parents are helping their children do homework and projects, which happens almost daily with elementary-aged children. Conversations about what they are learning at school can stimulate further teaching opportunities for parents.

Through personal interaction with children around educational material and topics, parents can help clarify their children's questions and positively influence and support their children's learning experiences. Many supplemental resources exist to support parents' at-home teaching of their children. These resources include, books, art, toys, games, and videos, all of which can be used to learn various educational concepts. By using these types of resources and actively engaging in discussion with their children, parents further fulfill their responsibility for their children's education.

As mentioned, a growing number of parents are choosing the homeschooling option each year. This rise may be related to issues and concerns about curricula. Homeschool parents are also interested in having more freedom of choice in regards to their children's daily environments and with their daily work schedules. Shannon and I both have many friends who homeschool their children, and we have much admiration for their commitment. They truly are invested at high levels in giving their children what they believe to be the best possible educational experiences. I have been impressed with the homeschooled children I have met across the country. I find them generally to be engaging in conversation and with strong social skills.

Homeschooling requires a high level of commitment on the part of parents. Usually, one of the parents is a stay-at-home parent-teacher and the other is highly involved when they come home from their work. One of the added advantages is the chance to take field trips that relate to what is being learned at home. Schedules can be much more flexible. This option also allows cooperation with other homeschooling parents who may have a high level of proficiency in a particular field of study.

These opportunities, as well as online classes, expose the child to teachers other than their parents. Some homeschooling parents also arrange for their children to take classes at private schools or local colleges in academic areas where the parent is not proficient. This tends to happen more at the middle school and high school levels.

If all of these choices seem overwhelming as you anticipate the arrival of your baby or look at your infant in the crib, don't be overly concerned. You have five years to think, explore, and decide what you will do when the time comes. In the meantime, let me remind you that children are learning every day, in every situation, so keep your eyes open and remind yourself that you are the primary educator of your child. While it may be true that in some ways "it takes a village to raise a child," parents are still ultimately responsible for finding and monitoring within the "village" the best care and best educational opportunities for their children.

Thankfully, others in the community want to partner with parents to help them and their children, but no one else in the community is going to care for a child at the same level and with the same love as parents. So, allow others to help you, but always keep in mind that no one is as important as you in the life of your child.

Talking It Over

1. For the first four to five years, you, your spouse, and whomever you choose as caregivers will greatly impact the future education of your child. What do you see as being the most important aspects of this preschool education?

2. Have you and your spouse discussed your options during these early educational years? Will there be a stay-at-home parent? Or will both of you follow your full-time vocational pursuits? Or will one of you be a part-time worker in order to have more time with your child?

3. If both of you plan to work full-time, whom have you chosen to care for your child while you are at work? Do you need to do further investigation into this topic?

4. I know you have five years to make this decision, but what are your present thoughts about where your child will attend kindergarten?

5. Reflect on your own formal education in elementary, middle school, and high school. What are your pleasant and not-so-pleasant memories? Share with each other your memories. How do you think these memories will influence your decision about the education of your child?

6. Remember, the culture in which we live is continually changing. Don't assume that the choice your parents made will be the right choice for your child. Discuss your present thoughts with your spouse.

7. Commit yourselves to taking the time to explore the various options thoroughly when the time comes for your child to begin formal education. It will be time well invested.

11

I Wish I'd Known . . .

That **MARRIAGES** *Do Not Thrive on* **AUTOPILOT**

Some time ago, a young man sat in my office and said, "I've lost my wife." "Do you mean she has left you?" I asked.

"Oh no, nothing like that. I mean that the baby has become the center of her life. It's like she is now a mother instead of a wife. I know the baby takes much of her energy, but how do we keep our marriage alive? I really do feel like I have lost my wife."

Over the years, I have heard similar complaints over and over again in my office. It may be a husband who feels that his wife is married to the baby, or a wife who feels that her husband is married to his job. One wife said, "He never helps me with the baby. When he comes home from work, he is on the computer getting ready for the next day. I think the baby needs a father as well as a mother. I know that I need his help. I feel so alone."

The reality is that after you have a child, your marriage will not thrive on autopilot. In chapter 1 we discussed how having a baby radically changes your schedule. In this chapter I want to share some practical ideas on how to keep your marriage alive while rearing a child. I am convinced that you can be good parents and have a healthy marriage.

It all begins with recognizing that things are different when you have a baby. You can't do things the way you've always done them. There are three of you now, instead of two, and one of the three needs vast amounts of attention from the other two. Yes, your "free time" will be much less than before. But don't buy into the idea that "there is just no time for us!" Surely there is a way to care for the baby's needs and love, encourage, and care for each other. After all, couples have been doing this for thousands of years. Some couples have three or more children and still have a good marriage. So what are some of the things that Shannon and I have learned through the years as we have counseled hundreds of couples?

How to have a growing marriage after the baby comes

Step one is *resolve*—by which I mean: determine, decide, and settle in your mind that "We will find a way to keep our marriage growing while we rear our child." This needs to be a conscious decision on the part of the husband and the wife; something you discuss and agree upon. Don't take it for granted. Verbalize your decision to each other. Seal it with a hug and a kiss! Now you are on the same page, headed in the same direction, with the will to succeed. Remember the old saying, "Where there's a will, there's a way."

If you have more children, you may need to renew your resolve from time to time because each additional child expands the workload. Shannon is honest about her own struggle. "Stephen and I found ourselves needing to assess our 'resolve' after several months of parenting three children. We vaguely remembered life before children and knew that we had been closer. Both working full-time and both fully engaged in parenting, we found ourselves having less time for one another. We didn't talk as much. We weren't as affectionate with one another. Sometimes we were unkind and spoke harshly. We were taking out life's frustrations on each other. We both knew something had to change. So, we had an honest, open conversation and renewed our resolve to make our marriage what we wanted it to be. That was a turning point for us. With resolve, we began to take steps to change our lifestyle."

If you have read any of my other books, you know that Karolyn and I had our own struggles in the early days of our marriage. It was "resolve" that kept us working on our marriage even when things seemed overwhelming. Maybe that is why I have so much hope for couples who are struggling. I know that if we, with all of our differences, learned to work as a team and create a loving, supportive relationship, so can others. Sometimes I say to couples in my office, "I understand that you have no hope. So, let's operate on my hope for you. I am not asking you to have hope, I'm asking you to 'resolve' to take steps to learn and change attitudes and actions, and let's see what happens." When couples have resolve they will create the marriage they've always wanted.

The birth of a baby will not solve the relationship problems that existed before the baby was born. Some couples think that "having a baby will draw us together." I do believe that when you look into the face of your baby there is an amazing sense that "we" have created this child. There is a psychological sense that "we are together on this journey." However, the birth of a child will not heal a broken relationship. It may create a realization that "we need to address our problems, not only for our own sake but also for the sake of our child." This motivation often leads couples to reach out for help. When a couple seeks help, they will find it.

Don't believe the common excuses that couples often make in our counseling offices. Here are some of the excuses we have heard: "I don't have enough time." "I don't have enough energy." "We don't have enough money." "She knows that I love her." "He is the problem, not me." "I will change when she changes." "We've tried before and are wasting our time by trying again." "We're really doing fine." "She is exaggerating our problems." By these and similar statements, couples are trying to excuse themselves for lack of "resolve" to work on their relationship. When you make such excuses, you become your worst enemy. I challenge you to take a "we can and we will" attitude. I promise, you will never regret the effort.

So, whether you have a healthy marriage or a struggling marriage, I hope you will find the ideas in this chapter helpful. Marriages are either growing or regressing. They never stand still. It is my desire that your marriage will grow, as together you give birth to a child and seek to be responsible parents.

Communication: marriage oxygen

Talking and listening—it seems so simple. Yet communication is to a marriage what oxygen is to the body. It keeps the marriage alive. When I know what my wife is thinking, what she has experienced today, and how she feels, I am better able to help and encourage her. But I will never know what is going on inside her unless she talks and I listen. Nor will she know my thoughts and feelings unless I reveal them by talking, and she chooses to listen.

That is why I recommend a "daily sharing time" in which you sit down and listen to each other. It may be only fifteen minutes, but at least you are checking in with each other daily. After this daily time of sharing life, I suggest you ask each other: "What can I do to help you?" After all, this is what marriage is all about; husband and wife helping each other reach their potential for good in the world. The old Hebrew adage says, "Two are better than one."[1] But that is true only if we have the attitude of helping each other.

I am not naive enough to think that all couples have this attitude—"How may I help you?" The reason I know this is not true is my own experience. Now don't get me wrong: when we were dating and I was caught up in the euphoria of being "in love," I would do anything for her. We seldom had arguments, because I really wanted to make her happy. What no one told me was that in approximately two years I would lose the "in-love" emotions. Then our differences would emerge and I would go back to being normal—that is to say, selfish. I started demanding things of her. That's when I found out that she too was selfish. She wanted her way as much as I wanted my way. Our marriage went from euphoric to desperate in a few months. I remember thinking, "I married the wrong person. This is not going to work out."

What compounded the problem for me was that I was in seminary studying to be a pastor. I was supposed to be this godly person, but I was anything but godly in my marriage. Things did not turn around until I got desperate enough to admit to God that I did not know how to save my marriage. When I asked God to show me, He did, but it was not what I expected. He reminded me that I was to be loving my wife "as Christ loved the church and gave himself up for her."[2] I knew that was not my attitude. In fact, my attitude was exactly the opposite; I wanted her to "give herself up for me."

> I was supposed to be this godly person, but I was anything but godly in my marriage.

When I admitted my own selfish attitude to God and later to Karolyn and asked forgiveness, things began to turn in a positive direction. I began to ask her three questions on a regular basis: How can I help you? How can I make your life easier? And, how can I be a better husband to you?" When I was willing to ask these questions, Karolyn was willing to give me answers. I was now committed to doing all I could to enrich her life. What happened is that within three months, she started asking me those three questions. When two people are genuinely seeking to enrich each other's life, they both become winners. That is what marriage was meant to be.

I believe that a daily sharing time in which you let each other into your experiences, thoughts, and feelings by talking and listening, coupled with an attitude of "How can I help you?", will lead to a growing marriage. So, if you don't already have a daily sharing time, I encourage you to start today. And, if you need to have an attitude change, I urge you to admit your selfishness to God and your spouse. I know God will forgive you, and I'm guessing that your spouse will also, especially when they begin to see your changed attitude.

Love is the opposite of selfishness. Love gives, while selfishness demands. Love seeks the well-being of the other, while selfishness seeks to satisfy my own needs. Two selfish people will never have a thriving marriage. Two loving people most definitely will.

Missing each other emotionally

So let's assume you are now on the road of love. Let me remind you of the five love languages, which we discussed in chapter 6. We learned that each child has an emotional love tank, which needs to be filled regularly by parents. I believe that adults also have an emotional "love tank." We too need to feel loved by the significant people in our lives. If we are married, the person we would most like to love us is our spouse. However, even when we are sincere in our love, we may be missing each other emotionally, because we have different love languages. He may be expressing his love by "acts of service," while her love language may be "quality time." So he does all kinds of things to help her and is shocked when she says, "I just don't feel like you love me." The problem is that he is speaking his love language and not hers. Over the past twenty years, I have helped thousands of couples discover each other's love language and change the emotional climate in their marriage. If you have not read my book *The 5 Love Languages: The Secret to Love That Lasts*, I would encourage you to read it together. The book has now sold over eleven million copies in English and been translated into fifty languages around the world. I believe it will greatly enhance your marriage.

Acknowledging your own selfishness, asking forgiveness, and then loving each other in the right love language creates a positive emotional atmosphere in the marriage. Life is much easier to process when the two of you feel loved and encouraged by the other. This does not mean that you will be perfect, but when you love each other, you will also apologize when you fail. I still sometimes say and do things that are hurtful, but when I realize that I have hurt my wife, I also am pained. This leads me to apologize, and hopefully she will forgive me. Again, there are no growing marriages without apology and forgiveness. Don't think that the passing of time will heal a fracture caused by hurtful behavior. Healing comes when the offender apologizes and the offended forgives.

Resolving conflicts

Keeping the "love tank" full and keeping the emotional barriers cleared away by apologizing and forgiving are two major elements of a thriving marriage. Another extremely important ingredient is learning to solve conflicts. Because we are human, and have different personalities, and backgrounds, we will sometimes have conflicts. By "conflict" I mean that we disagree and we both feel strongly about our position. All couples have conflicts. Some argue and fight, and others listen and look for solutions. I did my share of arguing and fighting in the early years. I much prefer listening and finding solutions. Unresolved conflicts create emotional distance between us. Resolving conflicts draws us together.

There are two key elements in resolving conflicts in a healthy manner. First, we must listen and try to understand the other person's position; not only what they think but what they are feeling. Try to put yourself in their shoes and look at the world through their eyes. Given their personality, and what they perceive to be the facts, can you understand how they might think what they think and feel what they feel? It is not that hard if you try. Then, express understanding. One of the most powerful things you can say, after listening, is "I can see how what you are saying makes sense." (And it always does make sense in their head.) When you say this, you are no longer the enemy but a friend who understands.

Then you can say, "Let me tell you how I'm looking at it, and see if you can understand my perspective." If your spouse listens with a view to understanding, he/she may also say, "I think I see where you are coming from and it makes sense. So, how can we solve this?" Now you can focus on looking for a solution rather than winning an argument.

Conflict can be resolved in one of three ways. (1) One of you agrees to move to the other's position. (2) You find a meeting place somewhere in the middle of the two ideas. (3) You agree to disagree and still be friends. Maybe in a few months you will be able to move to number one or two, but presently, you can accept the reality that you disagree, but will not let the issue divide you.

Some issues will remain as differences for a lifetime, but they need not be divisive. Karolyn and I have never agreed on how to load a dishwasher, but we have agreed to accept each other's method without getting bent out of shape. You may never agree on how to squeeze the toothpaste—middle or bottom, but you agree to get two tubes and each can squeeze in their own way. Personality differences will likely not change. So we must adjust to each other's patterns. Focus on the positive traits and minimize the things that irritate you. Life is too short to let our differences divide us.

In addition to these fundamental issues, Shannon and I would like to recommend the following:

Flirting, dating, and more

Flirt! Flirting or playfully engaging each other can spark excitement in the marriage. Do you remember how you flirted when you were dating? If so, you might imagine that you are dating again.

Date! In his book *52 Uncommon Dates*,[3] Randy Southern challenges couples to prioritize their married dating life. To help couples get their creative wheels turning, he recommends fifty-two fun and engaging dates that they can easily incorporate into their schedules if they will simply commit to do so. Thus, Southern gives couples the "what" and the "how"; couples then supply the "want to" and follow-through. Whether using *52 Uncommon Dates* or similar guides, or coming up with their own date ideas, couples who regularly prioritize date time stand to get great mileage out of dating that can help draw them closer together emotionally and physically. When the baby comes, you will need to find family or friends who will keep careful watch over the child so you can have a little time for each other. When the baby is an infant, you may have shorter dates, but as the child gets older, you can have extended dates.

Get physical! Little touches throughout the day; hugs, kisses, and handholding can be reminders that we value each other. These are especially meaningful to the spouse whose primary love language is physical touch. Touch communicates, "I want to be close to you." Yes, sexual intimacy is one dialect of physical touch, but not all touches need to lead to the bedroom. Certainly, a healthy sex life draws a couple emotionally closer together, but nonsexual touches are equally important for growing a healthy marriage.

Get away! I know some couples think, "We will never get a weekend away when the baby comes." Actually, the first year of the baby's life you can take the baby with you. I know it's not just the two of you, but you can care for the baby and focus on your relationship. As the baby gets older, you can get others to care for the baby while you are away. Even if it's only one night at a nice hotel or bed-and-breakfast, it can do wonders for your marriage. There is something about being together out of the house that invigorates the relationship.

Keep learning! Marriage is a lifelong journey. Don't ever think you have arrived. Stay open to learning. As long as we have life, we can and should be learning. Some things we learn by experience, but much is to be gained by exposing ourselves to what others have learned. I encourage couples to two lifelong practices. (1) Read and discuss one book on marriage every year. After reading each chapter, ask each other, "What can we learn from this chapter?" (2) Attend a marriage enrichment event once a year. This may be a weekend conference, a small retreat, a couple's night out, or a class offered in your church or community. From these events you will gain new perspectives, and creative ideas that will stimulate growth in your relationship.

Take care of yourself! Couples with young children can easily get caught up in the busyness of life and have little time for self-care. Keeping yourself physically, emotionally, and spiritually healthy is important not only for you but also for your marriage. What are your felt needs? Where do you need to give attention to yourself? What is available in your community that may help you? Many churches offer events that provide childcare so mothers can relax knowing that their child is in good hands while they focus on some activity that will enhance their own health.

> If you will decide now to prioritize your marriage, you will do your child a great service.

Couples can say "yes, but . . ." to any and all of these suggestions. However, if couples want to have thriving marriages, they must look for, create, and take every opportunity to enhance their relationship, even when, and especially when they have young children. By being proactive, couples have more control over their relationship than if they merely operate on "autopilot."

They are better able to face challenges that arise over time, and they increase their chances of having a healthy marriage. Couples who commit to growing their marriage relationship maximize their enjoyment of each other and will be better parents.

If you will decide now to prioritize your marriage, you will do your child a great service. Ultimately nothing is more important in parenting than to give your child a model of a mom and dad who love, encourage, and support each other; who process their conflicts in a positive manner; and who apologize and forgive each other when they fail. I hope that the ideas shared in this chapter will help you create that kind of marriage.

Talking It Over

1. Initiate a conversation with your spouse about keeping your marriage strong after the baby arrives. I hope you can land with "resolve"—"We will find a way to keep our marriage growing while we rear our child." Seal your "resolve" with a hug and a kiss.

2. If you are having unresolved issues in your relationship before the baby comes, I want to encourage you to talk with a counselor, pastor, or trusted friend now and seek to find solutions. It will be easier now than it will be after the baby arrives.

3. Establish a daily sharing time, in which you share with each other at least two things that happened in your life today and how you feel about it. Seek to understand and empathize with each other.

4. Begin the practice of asking each other daily, "What can I do to help you?"

5. Discover and speak each other's love language regularly. You may wish to take the free Love Language Profile found at *www.5lovelanguages.com*.

6. When you realize that you have failed to be loving, apologize and seek forgiveness. You may wish to read chapter 8 again.

7. When you have a conflict with your spouse, learn to say, "I know that we see this differently, so why don't we sit down and listen to each other. Would you like to go first? Or, would you like me to go first?" Concentrate on understanding your mate's position. Affirm them by saying, "I think I understand your side, and it makes sense." Then share your side. This kind of dialogue leads to solving conflicts.

8. Which of the following suggestions would you most like to do after you become parents? Rank each of these on a scale of 0–10 and share your answers.

____ Flirt

____ Date

____ Get physical

____ Get away

____ Keep learning

____ Take care of yourself

12

I Wish I'd Known . . .

That **CHILDREN**
Can Bring You **GREAT JOY**

n my mind, joy is more than a fleeting emotion. It is rather that deep underlying satisfaction with the way you are investing your life. Vocations that ultimately help people can be a source of joy. On the other hand vocations that are only for the purpose of earning money may bring little or no joy. Marriage itself can be a source of joy if it is the kind of marriage we described in chapter 11. Your relationship with your parents and extended family can bring joy if they are healthy relationships. Various recreational and social endeavors have the potential for stimulating joy if they are done with a wholesome attitude. However, few things can bring more joy than the investment you make in rearing children.

In previous chapters I have talked about sleepless nights,

messy diapers, potty training, occasional sickness, constant housecleaning, hectic schedules, and random acts of defiance. But in this chapter I want to talk about the joy that lies beneath all of these energy-draining challenges of parenting. Yes, child-rearing demands time, energy, money, and great effort, but the satisfaction far outweighs the stresses you experience on the journey.

The first sight of your newborn infant may be both terrifying and exhilarating. Terrifying because you feel inadequately prepared, but exhilarating because this is your baby. Together we have created a new human being. In this baby, though yet undeveloped, lies unlimited potential. You have the privilege and opportunity of teaching and training him/her to reach that potential. What could be more exciting and challenging?

As a dad, I am finding great joy in seeing my two grown children reaching their potential for God and good in the world. The good news is that you don't have to wait until they are well-trained adults to experience joy. Ask any older parent and they will tell you of the joy they experienced when they held and cuddled their infant while saying all those silly words, none of which the baby understood. They will also tell of the joy of rocking their baby to sleep, holding the hands of their toddler as he or she took their first steps, answering the questions of their inquisitive three- and four-year olds, crying when they left their child at kindergarten on the first day of school, or cheering with great enthusiasm for their elementary-aged child who scored one of the five baskets made by his or her team.

These joyful memories continue to bring deep satisfaction as children move on toward adulthood. Looking back, we sense how quickly the years of a child's development pass—or, putting it another way, "Those were long days and short years." What parents know is that the long days are soon forgotten, and the short years are long remembered.

Finding joy

Knowing that childhood doesn't last forever, how then do parents of young children focus on and celebrate the many joys of rearing children as opposed to getting overwhelmed in their various parenting responsibilities? That is the question that Shannon and I hope to answer in this chapter.

How's your health?

Let me begin by saying that your own emotional, mental, and spiritual health is the biggest factor in your finding joy in parenting. If you are not at peace with yourself, your spouse, and God, you may well see parenting as a burden rather than a joy.

So how do you measure your own health? One of the best measurement tools I have ever discovered was written in the first century by one of the early leaders in the Christian church. He suggested nine traits that will be present in a truly healthy person. They are: love, joy, peace, patience, kindness, goodness, faithfulness, gentleness, and self-control.[1] In my counseling I have found this to be a good diagnostic tool. To the degree that I am truly a loving person—have a genuine concern for others; have a deep satisfaction in how I am investing my life; am at peace with myself, God, and others; show patience, kindness, and goodness in all my relationships; am faithful; show persistence; am gentle in my approach to others; and control my passions and not let them control me—then to that degree, I am a healthy person.

I would challenge you to use this as a gauge of your mental,

> If you are not at peace with yourself, your spouse, and God, you may well see parenting as a burden rather than a joy.

emotional, and spiritual health. If you recognize the need for growth in some of these traits, then now would be a good time to read a book, talk to a friend, go for counseling, enroll in a class, talk with a pastor, get involved in a church, read the Scriptures, and pray. The Christian perspective is that God wants to give us the ability to actually become a fully healthy person. When you are this kind of person, you are more likely to truly experience joy on the parenting journey.

Finding joy in watching your child learn

One of the great joys in life is found in learning. I remember when I was a child and first began to find the excitement in reading books. It was such an adventure, the whole world opened up to me. It brought great satisfaction (joy). As parents we can experience this same kind of joy when we watch our children learn.

As we mentioned earlier, the child's learning process begins long before they go to school. Each step in learning basic motor skills can bring great joy to parents. A young father says to his wife, "Look, look, he just rolled over by himself. He was on his back and he rolled over on his stomach." In simply reading these words, you can sense the joy of this father. Then comes crawling and it's the mother's turn to say, "Look, look, he's crawling."

I still remember the excitement, the joy, of watching our children take their first steps. They were holding on to the couch. I would get eighteen inches away from them and say, "Come on. You can walk. Come on." They would take half a step and fall and I would say, "Yeah, let's try it again." I would put them back by the couch and repeat my challenge. One step, two steps, three steps, and before long they were walking. Every step brought joy to me as I watched them learning to walk.

It is not only the development of motor skills that bring joy but also learning the social skills about which we talked in chapter 9. When you hear your child say "please," or "thank you," without being coached, you will experience joy. Yes, the coaching was necessary, and perhaps took longer than you had planned, but your child got it. Oh, you may need to remind them from time to time, but they are on their way to learning two social skills that will enrich their relationships. So, as a parent, you can relax and experience a moment of joy. You and they are making progress.

Later will come academic progress, which can also bring joy to parents. When they learn to read, you will find yourself smiling. You have read books to them for a number of years, now they are reading books to you. The process is slow, but eventually they will read books and then share with you what they learned by reading. That's when you will say to your spouse, "I'm so glad that our children love to read books." You know that if children are readers, their world will continue to expand, and that brings you great joy.

When you see them learn to take initiative in completing their homework and household chores before going out to play, you will sense another round of deep satisfaction. You know that learning to prioritize life—doing the most important things first—will enhance their relationships when they become adults.

Yes, there is great joy in watching your child learn the skills and attitudes that will lead them to being responsible adults. When parents reflect on this truth, they may feel less overwhelmed by the time and practice that learning requires, and more hopeful about the lasting results their efforts will have. This attitude will help parents breathe a little easier and capture the many joys related to the child's learning process.

Parents who are enjoying their child's learning journey may also rediscover the joy of learning themselves. While reading books to your young children, you may be reminded of some of the lessons you learned as a child. For example, the classic story *The Little Engine That Could* has a lesson for adults as well as for children. Or, if your parents did not read to you, in reading to your children, you may discover the joy of reading. As you watch select television programs with your children and then ask, "What can we learn from this program?" you may learn as much as your child, or sometimes even more than your child. Rearing children often stimulates parents to reengage in the process of learning. We are never too old to learn.

Creating joyful experiences

Parents also experience joy by creating joyful experiences for their children. I think that most parents want home to be a joyful place, a safe haven from the pressures outside the home. We want this for ourselves, and we want it for our children. One approach to making this a reality is to ask the question: When my children are grown, what do I hope they will most remember about our family?

Perhaps if you asked yourself that question, you might find your mind returning to your own childhood, especially if you had a wholesome childhood. For example, you may remember that your parents read stories with you every night before bed, and perhaps prayed with you. You may remember that they attended every ball game or other school activity in which you were involved.

Perhaps they taught you to play the piano or guitar or how to sew. What positive memories do you have of childhood that may be things you would like to do for and with your children?

Of course, not all adults grew up in a positive, joyful home. Some grew up afraid, in a home filled with harsh, hurtful words and unpredictable outbursts. So if you don't have positive childhood memories, then it is time to be creative. Think and talk with your spouse about the kind of memories you want for your children. What do you hope they will say about your family when they are adults?

Here are some of the positive statements that parents have shared with Shannon and me through the years. "My parents always made time for me." "We read books." "We built stuff together." "We played outside." "We always prayed before dinner." "We laughed all the time." "We went to church every Sunday." "We sang together." Perhaps these may be some of the things you want your children to remember.

As I noted earlier, both of our children are grown and married. When they reflect on their childhood, they tell us that two of their favorite memories focused on meals. When our first child was old enough to eat at the table, Karolyn made the decision to cook a hot breakfast for the family every morning. Now, Karolyn is not a morning person. So, this was a Mother Teresa–type decision for her. She did this until our youngest went off to college. I agreed that I would read from the Scriptures and have prayer every morning while we were seated at the table. As the children got older, I let them pray if they wished. Sometimes we did this before Karolyn served the food and sometimes after. It was always brief, but I hoped meaningful.

As the children grew old enough to participate in conversation, we used the dinner meal as a time to share what had happened in our lives throughout the day. We would commend the children for the kind things they did, and question the things that did not sound very kind. Karolyn and I shared both our successes and failures as well. We followed this practice through middle school and high school. (We had to shift mealtimes, earlier or later, when our son was playing basketball.) We believed that our evening mealtime was an important opportunity to stay in touch with each other. Our topics of discussion got broader and deeper in the high school years.

Both of our children look back and say that our morning and evening mealtimes are some of their fondest memories. When they would bring friends home from college, we continued our mealtime discussions. Many of their friends were amazed that families actually talked with each other.

Now is the time to decide how you as parents will make your home life a positive experience for your child. I know that life is busy, but what could be more important than equipping your children to find their way in life, contribute to society in unique and important ways, and some day effectively build their own family relationships? Neither Shannon nor I have ever heard anyone say, "I wish I had cleaned my house more often when my children were growing up." "I wish I had worked more." "I wish we had spent less time together." No! Parents instead say the opposite. They wish they had prioritized time with their children and done more things they enjoyed with their children.

> Childhood is fleeting, so parents are wise to think earlier rather than later about their desired parenting outcomes.

Parents sometimes know with more clarity later on in life

what they wished they had done differently as younger parents. But childhood is fleeting, so parents are wise to think earlier rather than later about their desired parenting outcomes. This can help them fully create and engage in joyful relationships with their children.

Finding joy in play

One other huge source of joy for parents is in playing with their children. Play comes naturally for children. Through play, children express themselves, explore the world around them, solve problems, connect with others, and build valuable life skills. Thus, play provides wonderful opportunities for parents to connect with, understand, and encourage their children. In so doing, parents find great joy.

The challenge for parents is making time for play when they are busy with so many other responsibilities and interests. Again, the key word is *prioritize*. Play is one of the most important sources of joy for your child. Why put off today what you may not be able to do tomorrow? Or, why put off today what you will not be able to do a few years from now? Don't set yourself up for regrets! Make time now to play with your children.

When parents fully engage in play, they will likely remember just how much fun it is to play. Children will remind them of the endless possibilities of play—dress-up, tea parties, pirate sword-fights, Matchbox car races, building towers, building forts, having snowball fights, board games, video games, Legos, musical duets, dance parties, and comedy routines. Then there are basketball games in the driveway, Wiffle Ball home-run derbies, tag, and hide-and-seek. Through these and so many other activities, children invite their parents to play and welcome invitations from their parents to play. As they interact in these fun and creative ways, parents and children enjoy each other and draw closer together. In fact, their playtime and leisure time may be some of their most joyful family memories in the future.

Not only is joy found in playing with your children but also in watching your children play with others. Whether it is organized sports or playing with neighborhood kids in the backyard, when you see your child demonstrating good sportsmanship and having fun, you will likely feel a sense of pleasure.

However, I do want to share one warning about organized sports—don't take the game too seriously. I have seen parents get angry with their child or the coach and demonstrate un-sportsmanlike conduct themselves. This takes all the joy out of sports. Better to accept the fact that things will not always go as you wish. Affirm your child's efforts and by your own behavior help them learn to accept the authorities' call, even when you disagree with it.

Finding joy in expressing appreciation

In all the ways that you will spend time with and enjoy your child, look for opportunities to express appreciation to your child. If you did not grow up in a home that was supportive, don't let that keep you from giving to your child what you did not receive. You can learn from a negative parental example as well as a positive example. Ask yourself: What did my parents do or fail to do that I would like to do differently? On the other hand, if you grew up with loving, supportive, caring parents, ask yourself: What did my parents do that I would like to emulate? And, what might I do to build upon their example?

Children crave and deserve affirmation from their parents.

Your words of encouragement will bring them great joy. I don't mean that you cannot correct your children for poor behavior. We discussed the value of discipline in chapter 5. However, discipline should be given in love, never in anger. When children feel loved and affirmed, they are far more likely to bring their parents deep satisfaction. When parents are harsh and condemning, and children feel unloved and rejected, their behavior is not likely to bring joy to the parents. That is why I have to admit in this chapter on "children can bring you great joy" that children can also bring you great pain.

So many parents have sat in my and Shannon's offices deeply pained by the decisions and behavior of their teenage son or daughter. They look back over the brief years of their

> Ask yourself: What did my parents do or fail to do that I would like to do differently?

childhood and say, "We wish we could go back. So many things we would do differently." Shannon and I hope that this chapter will help you live without regrets. If you enjoy your children, chances are they will enjoy being your children and will bring you great joy.

If you focus on the challenges and stresses of parenting, joy may take flight. But if you focus on the joy that children bring, and make the most of each day, joy will be your constant companion.

Talking It Over

1. In what ways do you think you brought joy to your parents when you were a child?

2. In what ways do you think you brought pain to your parents?

3. How do you think your childhood will affect your parenting?

4. In what ways do you wish to emulate what your parents did?

5. In what ways do you wish to parent differently?

6. What books did you read as a child? What books do you plan to read to your child?

7. What games did you enjoy playing with your parents, siblings, or peers? Can you envision playing those games with your child?

8. How do you assess your own emotional, mental, and spiritual health based on the nine-point diagnostic tool we discussed earlier? Rate yourself on a scale of 0–10 on each of the following traits:

_____ Love

_____ Joy

_____ Peace

_____ Patience

_____ Kindness

_____ Goodness

_____ Faithfulness

_____ Gentleness

_____ Self-control

What can you do now to cultivate these traits in your life in preparation for parenting?

Epilogue

I think that most people would agree that the basic unit of human society is the family. As I mentioned earlier, my educational journey includes a bachelor and master's degree in cultural anthropology. It is a universal reality that family—mom, dad, and children—is viewed as the fundamental building block of all societies. Each culture may have a different language and may have various other social structures, but the family is the one social unit that unites all cultures.

When the family is healthy, children grow up equipped to be responsible adults. When the family is unhealthy, children grow up with many internal struggles, and as adults may have difficulty in forming healthy relationships. As a father, I can think of few things that would be more painful than to rear children who come to adulthood ill prepared. That is why I have devoted my life to helping husbands and wives have healthy marriages and become responsible parents.

This book is another effort on my part, with the help of Dr. Shannon Warden, to give the parents of this generation some of the insights I have learned as a parent, a counselor, and a lifelong student of marriage and family. I have sought to give a realistic picture of the challenges and stresses of parenting, along with practical ideas on how to create a positive family climate in today's shifting culture.

What I have shared are insights I sincerely wish someone would have told me before we had children. Karolyn and I agree that had we known these things then, we would have been better parents. Many of these things we eventually learned, but we learned the hard way—by experience. My hope is that couples who read this book before the baby arrives will be much better prepared than we were.

I also hope that this book will be a handy reference for parents as the child moves through the developmental stages of growth, physically, mentally, emotionally, socially, and spiritually. That is, I hope this will not be a "one read" book but that parents will turn to it again and again on the parenting journey.

Shannon shared a list of things that she and Stephen have agreed upon that have made parenting less stressful for them. You will see many of the ideas in this book reflected in their list.

- We expect and accept that our children require a lot of our time.
- We remember that we desperately wanted each of these precious children.

- We trust that God gives us all the time we need to do everything we need to do.
- We prioritize our children and their well-being above our personal and professional interests.
- We reach out for help from trusted caregivers like our parents.
- We play with the kids often because we know they won't be little forever.
- We consider our children's developmental stages and schedule activities such that we do not stress our children beyond their limits.
- We divide and conquer whenever possible, such that one of us is tending to one or two children while the other is helping do things like homework or baths.
- We take breaks from extracurricular activities (ours and the children's) so that we are not overscheduling our family time.
- We avoid places such as busy restaurants where our children will be overstimulated and hard to manage.
- We laugh about how we will go to restaurants one day and be bored without small children to disrupt our meal.
- We celebrate small parenting successes and know that these are signs of good things to come for our children.
- We want to—and know that—we must constantly tend to our marriage relationship so that it does not get sidetracked by our parenting and other responsibilities.
- We expect and accept the reality that we will go to bed very tired and wake up at least a little less tired.

Shannon and Stephen are still in the process of rearing their three children. Karolyn and I have reared our children and now have grandchildren. To be honest, I like this stage of life. But, to be honest, I liked every stage. Yes, there were hard times. There were times when I prayed for wisdom I did not have . . . and received it. Looking back, the hard times don't stand out in my mind. What I remember are the joys of seeing our daughter and son develop their abilities. I enjoyed every basketball game and every piano recital. Did I have to adjust my schedule? Yes, but it was worth it.

Now that our children are grown and married, Karolyn and I find great joy in seeing how they are investing in their marriages, and how they are investing their vocational lives in helping others. And, yes, we take great joy in seeing our grandchildren reading, studying, playing, and honoring their parents and grandparents. I fully agree with one of the apostles in the early Christian church who said, "I have no greater joy than to hear that my children are walking in the truth."[1]

Shannon and I hope you have found this book helpful. If so, please recommend it to your friends. We welcome your feedback and suggestions at *www.5lovelanguages.com.*

GARY CHAPMAN

Notes

INTRODUCTION
1. US Department of Health and Human Services Office on Women's Health (2009). Infertility fact sheet accessed at http://www.womenshealth.gov/publications/our-publications/fact-sheet/infertility.html#1.

CHAPTER ONE
That Having Children Radically Changes Your Schedule
1. Gary Chapman, *The 5 Love Languages* (Chicago: Northfield Publishing, 2015).

CHAPTER TWO
That Children Are Expensive
1. Lino, Mark (2014). The United States Department of Agriculture's Center for Nutrition Policy and Promotion (CNPP) report entitled: "Expenditures on Children by Families."
2. Gary Chapman and Arlene Pellicane, *Growing Up Social* (Chicago: Northfield Publishing, 2014).

CHAPTER FIVE
That Children Need Boundaries
1. Rudolf Dreikurs, *Children: The Challenge* (New York: Hawthorn/Dutton, 1964).
2. Gary Chapman and Ross Campbell, *The 5 Love Languages of Children* (Chicago: Northfield Publishing, 2012).

CHAPTER SIX
That Children's Emotional Health Is as Important as Physical Health
1. John Bowlby, *A Secure Base: Parent-Child Attachment and Healthy Human Development* (New York: Basic Books, 1988).
2. Erik H. Erikson, *Childhood and Society* (New York: Norton, 1964).
3. Chapman and Campbell, *The 5 Love Languages of Children*.

CHAPTER SEVEN
That Children Are Greatly Influenced by Our Model
1. Brian Gene White, Rodney A. Atkins, & Steven A. Dean, "Watching You" (recorded by Rodney Atkins). On *If You're Going Through Hell* (CD) (Nashville: Curb Records, 2006).

CHAPTER EIGHT
That Sometimes Parents Need to Apologize
1. Gary Chapman and Jennifer Thomas, *When Sorry Isn't Enough* (Chicago: Northfield Publishing, 2013).

CHAPTER NINE
That Social Skills Are as Important as Academic Skills
1. George Sweeting, *Who Said That?* (Chicago: Moody Publishers, 1995), 250.
2. American Academy of Pediatrics, "Policy Statement: Media Use by Children Younger than 2 Years," American Academy of Pediatrics (2011), http://pediatrics.aappublications.org.
3. Gary Chapman, *Love as a Way of Life* (Colorado Springs: WaterBrook Press, 2008), 103.
4. Gary Chapman, *Anger: Taming a Powerful Emotion* (Chicago: Northfield Publishing, 2015).

CHAPTER ELEVEN
That Marriages Do Not Thrive on Autopilot
1. Ecclesiastes 4:9.
2. Ephesians 5:25.
3. Randy Southern, *52 Uncommon Dates* (Chicago: Moody Publishers, 2014).

CHAPTER TWELVE
That Children Can Bring You Great Joy
1. Galatians 5:22–23.

EPILOGUE
1. 3 John 4.

Acknowledgments

We would first of all like to thank our spouses, Karolyn Chapman and Stephen Warden. Their help and encouragement made it possible for us to have the time and energy to complete this project.

The couples who have sat in our counseling offices and shared their parenting successes and struggles have also greatly shaped our understanding of parenting. For this we are deeply grateful.

We are very appreciative of the many hours invested by Anita Hall, who not only computerized the manuscript but made helpful suggestions.

The Moody Publishers team have done their usual excellent job of encouraging, supporting, and guiding our efforts. Betsey Newenhuyse assisted greatly with her editorial suggestions. John Hinkley has been our constant advisor and encourager.

IMPROVING MILLIONS OF MARRIAGES
ONE LANGUAGE AT A TIME.

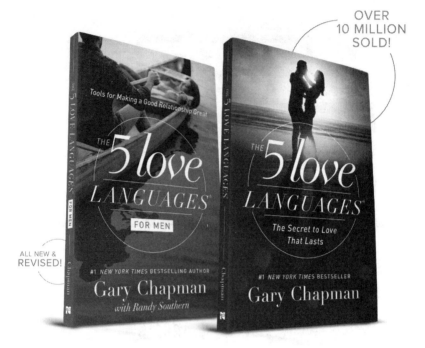

SPEAK YOUR CHILD'S LOVE LANGUAGE IN A WAY THAT HE OR SHE UNDERSTANDS.

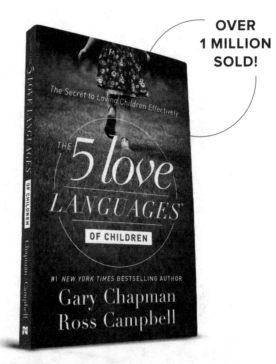

EVERY CHILD has a unique way of feeling loved. When you discover your child's love language—and how to speak it—you can build a solid foundation for your child to trust you and flourish as they grow.

In this book for parents, teachers, single parents, and more, Drs. Gary Chapman and Ross Campbell offer practical advice for how to:

- Discover and speak your child's love language—in dozens of ways!
- Use the love languages to help your child learn best
- Discipline and correct more lovingly and effectively

INCLUDES THE LOVE LANGUAGE MYSTERY GAME FOR CHILDREN

WWW.5LOVELANGUAGES.COM

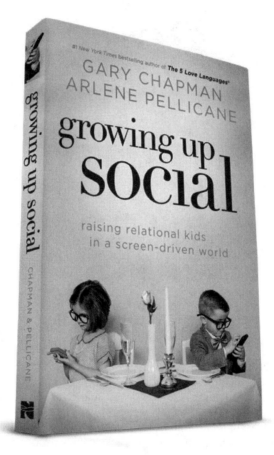

You're ready for kids, now strengthen their foundation: your marriage.

The stakes on marriage are high, but the rewards of preparing are even higher. Whether you're single or dating, this book can be your relationship blueprint and help you decide if and when you're ready to tie the knot. If you're engaged, even recently married, it will help you examine your relationship foundation and learn the skills necessary for building a successful marriage.

ALSO AVAILABLE AS AN EBOOK

MOODY Publishers®

From the Word to Life®